"The 'Problem of Evil' in a world created and maintained by an all-powerful and all-loving God has perplexed theologians and philosophers for ages. Not only have high thinkers grappled with it, but millions of the so-called 'common people' have felt heartbreak when languishing under the pain of evil and suffering. From the sage to the serf, from the philosopher to the pauper, from the theologian to the tradesman, all have bitterly cried out 'Why?' In Dr. DiCello's book, all of the answers are not given. This is to be expected. No simple, pat answers here. Dr. DiCello challenges us to view the 'Problem of Evil' from a balanced biblical worldview. His insights drawn from Scripture give us some answers but mostly they draw us into a deeper sense of awe for our all-powerful and all-loving God."

–Rick Walston
President, Columbia Evangelical Seminary

Why?

Why?
Reflections on the Problem of Evil

❧

Carmen C. DiCello

Wipf & Stock Publishers
Eugene, Oregon

WHY? REFLECTIONS ON THE PROBLEM OF EVIL

Wipf & Stock Publishers
199 W. 8th Ave., Suite 3
Eugene, OR 97401

ISBN 13: 978-1-4982-4899-0

For all who,
when intellectually perplexed or emotionally scarred,
have dared to ask,
"Why?"

Contents

Acknowledgments   xi

Chapter 1 – Introduction   3

Chapter 2 – Preliminary Remarks   7

Chapter 3 – Categories of Inquiry   15

    Excursus: When Skeptics Ask   21

Chapter 4 – Partial (Yet Incomplete) Explanations for Evil   25

Chapter 5 – Pieces of the Puzzle: Seeking a
Biblical Perspective on Evil   37

    Excursus: Is it Ever Right to Complain?   43

Chapter 6 – Job, the Invisible World, and Evil   47

Chapter 7 – Compatibilism and Divine Mystery   53

Chapter 8 – Jesus–Theodicy and Hope   61

Chapter 9 – Coping with Evil   69

Chapter 10 – Evil in a Postmodern Era   77

Chapter 11 – Conclusion   87

Appendix A – I Peter 3:15 and an Apologetic of Hope   93

Appendix B – Additional Musings on the Proper
Response to Mystery   95

Appendix C – Is Evil Really a Mystery?   97

Appendix D – Thoughts on Personal Evil   103

Appendix E – God and Tsunami   105

Bibliography   113

Credits   117

Acknowledgements

A number of people played a vital role in the completion of this manuscript. Many thanks to Dr. Rick Walston, who proofread and offered suggestions along the way. Mark "Moke" DiCello has for years been a conversation partner in discussing this puzzling subject. Mary Kay Walsh, another like-minded friend, has always been an encouragement. Bruno Tassone is always there to listen and share helpful thoughts (KP!). Robert "Bib" Porter, who overcame many difficulties on his way to completing his college degree, is a good friend. My students at Pottsville Area High School have been a constant source of motivation, reminding me each day of the joys and struggles of life in the real world.

Also, I would like to thank Steve Gunderson, Jason Crowder, and John Smulo, along with Dr. Walston mentioned above, for their willingness to endorse this project. Your assistance and kind words are greatly appreciated.

I am very grateful for the diligent efforts of a number of people without whose help and expertise this manuscript would never have been brought to print. Natalie Giboney of FreelancePermissions.com acquired permissions. Kimberly Medgyesy provided the typesetting, and the good people at Wipf & Stock worked patiently with me throughout the publication process. All of your efforts have been substantial and very much appreciated.

Above all, I want to thank my tremendous wife, Marilyn, and my fabulous kids, Luke and Jake. Thanks for enduring my seemingly endless hours in front of the computer. You guys are an immense gift and the joy of my life. More than anyone else, you enable me to "hear the music" that God is playing each day.

*"Although the world is full of suffering,
it is also full of the overcoming of it."*

Helen Keller

Chapter 1

Introduction

A child is abandoned, an elderly man mistreated, a disease interferes with an otherwise healthy home, massive numbers of people starve, a woman is brutally abused, senseless killings take place–the amount of suffering in this world is staggering, and when experienced, justice seems a trite concept and comfort an unrealistic ideal. Human experience is truly dominated by pain, sickness, and calamity. Indeed, however successful a person might be at evading trouble, the greatest enemy of all, death,[1] eventually swallows its prey like a dark gapping abyss. As a result, sadness and confusion plague every generation.

All people struggle with life in a nefarious world. For theists, not the least Christian theists, evil's presence is a baffling reality. Theologians and philosophers, long recognizing such widespread maleficence as a stumbling block to faith, have termed this subject *the problem of evil*. While much

---

[1] In one sense death is the ultimate example of evil, of what ought *not* occur. But since sin has entered the world, it also serves a good purpose. Blocher says, "death (of a man) is evil because God did not desire it, in the sense of Ezekiel 18:32; but *once sin has appeared*, death is something good in terms of its relationship to justice." Henri Blocher, *Evil and the Cross* (Downers Grove: InterVarsity Press, 1994), 88. Death, then, is something quite unnatural, a bad thing, but it is used as a means to something good, i.e., divine justice.

good transpires in this world, often it is outmatched (or at least outlasted) by trials and the many faces of misery. Clearly, in both philosophical and practical ways, evil is not easily explained.[2]

Therefore, in light of evil's devastating record, all conscientious Christians would do well to inquire as to why an all-good, all-powerful God allows such atrocity and anguish. Emotional solace and intellectual integrity demand nothing less than a serious appraisal of these matters.

> Why did God not remove evil from the world in a single stroke? Why did he not prevent it from perfecting its methods, to the misery of so many human beings? Why did he allow the devil time to counter-offense, with all the allurements of a false Christianity? We do not have access to the counsel of God to explain all of his ways. If the answer is part of "the secret things" that "belong to the Lord God" (Dt. 29:29), we shall submit without demur; but if "the things revealed" throw any light on the questions, then it is our duty to gather from there what we can.[3]

While an exhaustive and universally satisfying theodicy[4] may be unrealistic, a biblical perspective on evil should enliven faith and promote stability and worship. To that end, the aim here will be to provide a framework for understanding the problem of evil.[5]

---

[2]"What do people mean, when in a real-life situation they use the word 'evil'? They are talking about its *unjustified reality*. In common parlance, evil is 'something' that occurs in experience and *ought not to*." Ibid., 10.

[3]Ibid., 125.

[4]A theodicy is an attempt to explain the presence of evil in a good and sovereign God's world. Feinberg states it this way: "The ways of God are defensible, and they are defensible in such a way that no theist should have to give in to the charge of irrationality due to a problem of evil." J. S. Feinberg, "Theodicy" in *Evangelical Dictionary of Theology*, ed. Walter A. Elwell (Grand Rapids: Baker Books, 1984), 1086.

[5]A distinction is usually made between moral and natural evil. See John G. Stackhouse, Jr., *Can God Be Trusted: Faith and the Challenge of Evil* (New York: Oxford University Press, 1998), 30-44.

*"This is not a perfect world.
In a perfect world, evil loses."*

Anonymous

❧

Chapter 2

Preliminary Remarks

When dealing with a topic of this magnitude and complexity, it is worthwhile to consider the hopes and limitations of such an effort. All too often unnecessary distractions, questions, and speculations detract from the overall goal of a project. Perhaps, some of these can be avoided by clearly delineating factors that influence any attempt to construct a theodicy. These remarks are intended to provide general parameters and presuppositions for this study.

1. It is impossible to make any sense of evil apart from a God-given, universal norm.

The existence of evil has long been considered an argument against theism. If there is evil, God—at least an omnipotent, omnibenevolent God—cannot exist. Yet, this is hardly a valid position, for one cannot even define evil, or distinguish it from good, apart from a universal standard. On the other hand, the recognition of evil, i.e., that certain things are unequivocally wrong, assumes such a standard.

Of course there have been many attempts to construct a moral code based on human experience, observation, or a vague sense of spirituality. There are even some who are willing to take atheism to its logical extreme, recognizing that a universe void of God is one in which an absolute ethic cannot be maintained; thus, man's sense of morality must be explained in terms of biological or social evolution, or some other factor.

Few, however, take this route, and most who believe that there are no absolutes still live as if they exist. In fact all non-theistic explanations of morality are inadequate; those who try to manufacture them find it quite difficult to define what moral code should be followed and why it is to be preferred over some other option. Indeed, it is difficult to imagine how anyone might come up with a certain basis of morality, an "ought," apart from a universal Law-Giver. "Without this God who is sovereign and good, what is the rationale of our complaints? Can we even tell what is evil?"[6] Yancey correctly notes that

> belief in evil offers a backhand proof of God's existence. Indeed, the very outrage we feel at evil acts–hijackers steering jet planes into buildings full of citizens, concentration camp guards torturing their prisoners, kidnappers abusing and killing young children–points to a built-in sense that some things are desperately wrong, blameworthy, damnable.[7]

In other words the fact that there is evil and that it is generally identifiable, demands belief in a Creator. Otherwise, it makes no sense to complain. This is why a theistic position is the only way ahead. What all people who suffer[8] yearn for, and what all intellectuals desire, is something more than human opinion and conjecture.

---

[6]Henri Blocher, *Evil and the Cross*, 102-103.

[7]Philip Yancey, *Rumors of Another World: What on Earth Are We Missing?* (Grand Rapids, MI: Zondervan Publishing House, 2003), 114.

[8]*Evil* is something that ought not be, while *suffering* is that which normally proceeds from one's experience of evil. While they are not technically equivalent terms, they are both used here to refer to this basic fact: God allows bad things (i.e., evil) to touch our lives. Of course not all suffering is the result of evil in the world. Sometimes, suffering is self-imposed, resulting from wrong choices (we do something wrong) or inaccurate perceptions (we misinterpret our circumstances).

Only a Supreme Being can provide reliable and universally applicable standards.[9] Of course this does not clear up the problem of evil. It does, however, defeat the notion that evil's presence proves the non-existence of God, for evil cannot be in the least sense explained or opposed unless there is a morality-making deity, a God who has spoken.

> Human thinking must be subject to a norm, to a criterion. If we reject God as the norm, we must find another (rationalism) or despair entirely of knowledge (skepticism). Rationalism brings intellectual bondage to human systems, and skepticism is intellectual death. When we serve God, however, our minds are set free from human traditions and from the death of skepticism to accomplish their great tasks.[10]

Far from limiting intellectual pursuits, a biblical worldview provides the basis for making sense of life, including the mysteries. As Scripture says, "Your word is a lamp to my feet and a light to my path" (Psalm 119:105) and "The unfolding of Your words gives light; It gives understanding to the simple" (Psalm 119:130). Christianity asserts that one of God's clearest vehicles of communication is His Word. Those who seek Him there discover that "the fear of the Lord is the beginning of knowledge" (Proverbs 1:7).

---

[9]Many of those who flippantly deny or doubt God's existence are less apt to follow through on the implications of atheism. When a skeptic's house is vandalized, or an atheist is raped, the instinctive response is the same: "That's wrong!" "Indeed, one will probably never find an atheist who lives consistently with his system. For a universe without moral accountability and devoid of value is unimaginably terrible." William Lane Craig, *Reasonable Faith: Christian Truth and Apologetics* (Wheaton, IL: Crossway Books, 1994), 68. Thus, the atheist's or agonistic's philosophy is impossible to sustain in the real world. The Bible predicts this, declaring that humans have an innate, albeit marred, knowledge of God and His ways (see Romans 1:19-22).

[10]John M. Frame, *The Doctrine of the Knowledge of God* (Phillipsburg, NJ: Presbyterian and Reformed Publishing Company, 1987), 124-125.

2. Part of the difficulty in understanding evil is due to the fact that all of us are limited, both by our humanity and by our depravity.

None of us possesses the capacity of unlimited choice. Thus, our admiration of the bird's ability to defy gravity does not thereby equip us with the ability to fly. So it is when it comes to our comprehension of the Creator. We are simply limited when it comes to understanding God, whose thoughts and ways are often inscrutable (Deuteronomy 29:29; Isaiah 55:8-9). Thus, the Psalmist asks this rhetorical question: "Who is like the LORD our God, Who is enthroned on high, Who humbles Himself to behold the things that are in heaven and in the earth?" (Psalm 113:5-6). No one is like the Lord, which is precisely the point. Many things about "the high and lofty One" (Isaiah 57:15) will always defy our human categorizations.

This is further complicated by human corruption, which contributes to man's ignorance. Man's thinking processes are marred and unable to function with precision. We are thus described in terms of weakness (Romans 6:19; 8:26; 2 Corinthians 11:30), pride (Proverbs 29:23; 1 John 2:16), ignorance (1 Peter 1:14), and foolishness (Galatians 3:3; Ephesians 5:17), being liable to deception (2 Corinthians 11:3; Galatians 6:7). Indeed, even those who are united with their Creator and recipients of spiritual renovation (John 3:3; 1 Peter 1:3, 23) are far from grasping the divine mind *in toto*.

These factors—creaturehood and moral/spiritual impairment—surely contribute to the worldwide inability to make sense of so many things. These limitations and flaws render us incapable of solving these dilemmas entirely.

3. In response to those who in the presence of evil choose to react against God, it is important to keep in mind that God is not ultimately accountable to His creatures.

In the effort to grasp the mysteries of God's world, it is essential to recognize whose world it is. Certainly, the potter has the right to do what he chooses with his own clay (Romans 9:21). God can do what He wants with that which is His, and everything is His! This is the answer to those who are determined to reject divine sovereignty.

As mentioned earlier, God alone, since He is the Creator-Redeemer, is able to illumine mankind's path. Though the Lord has given a measure of intuition to all people, the final measuring stick of morality and guide to spirituality is His inscribed Word. There we discover that God's wisdom and ways must take precedence, even over human attempts to understand.

Though often hurt and mystified by the presence of evil, it is necessary to follow Scripture's counsel and to bow with Job who said, "I have declared that which I did not understand, things too wonderful for me, which I did not know . . . Therefore I retract, and I repent in dust and ashes" (Job 42:3. 6). As Frame points out:

> In God's decisions, he will not submit to man's judgment. He reserves the right to behave in a way that may offend human values, that may even appear, from a human viewpoint, to contradict His own values. And when that happens, He is not under man's judgment. He is not obligated to explain.[11]

4. Whatever else is true, the God of Scripture is always portrayed as a being of immeasurable love, compassion, and grace.

It is important to recognize this fact, especially when confronted with personal dilemmas and intellectual struggles that can, quite frankly, rattle our faith and make us wonder what type of deity He is. The assumption made here is that even in the face of evil and pain God is good, compassionate, and kind. Though we cannot deny the problem of evil, we must never renounce our commitment to the fundamental reality that "God is love" (1 John 4:8).

---

[11]John M. Frame, *Apologetics to the Glory of God: An Introduction* (Phillipsburg, NJ: Presbyterian & Reformed Publishing Company, 1994), 172.

Conclusion

The purpose of these preliminary remarks is to provide a basis for a theodicy. Though other factors might be mentioned, the principles noted here represent a substantial starting point. Any Christian approach to the problem of evil must begin with a commitment to God's Word in Scripture, a recognition of human limitations, a concomitant understanding of God's greatness, a proper reverence for the sovereignty of God, and a belief that, whatever else is true, God is and always will be nothing less than the eternal paradigm of love.

"The kind of certainty proper to a human being will be one which rests on the fidelity of God, not upon the competence of the human knower."

Lesslie Newbigin

❧

Chapter 3

Categories of Inquiry[12]

When considering the hurt and doubt engendered by the presence of evil, it is important to be aware of the various motivations for people's questions. Some think of evil as an intellectual difficulty, a cognitive puzzle. For others, however, evil is a felt reality, something which directly or indirectly affects lives; these individuals are not so much intellectually stumped, as they are emotionally crushed.

Because of the wide range of responses to suffering and pain, the apologist's emphasis and counsel must be geared to the individual. While it is obviously impossible to categorize every potential reaction to adversity, it is helpful to think through some of the general reasons why people complain. Here, then, is a list of some of the typical inquirers and a response to each.

1. The Insurrectionist: A Mutinous Heart

The first objection comes from those who are antagonistic. This group consists of individuals who are at some level opposed to God and His

---

[12]These categories are applicable to both Christian and non-Christian inquirers. Likewise, the general counsel suggested relates to all people.

ways. A portion of these is the intellectual or pseudo-intellectual type, specializing in well-constructed (or not-so-well-constructed) arguments against theism in general and Christianity in particular. Others are everyday folk, who have grown bitter because of a frowning providence. Included here, as well, are believers who, perhaps due to tragedy, blame God for the evil they encounter and turn their frustration and anger toward Him.

Since this is a common reaction, it is important to be alert to such hostility. While we should make every effort to avoid simplistic solutions, one primary strategy is to directly challenge rebellion. One person who learned this lesson was Job. Though generally faithful, Job eventually succumbed to a type of arrogant complaining. As a result, he received a visitation from the transcendent Lord, whose divine counsel is sobering. God asks, "Where were you when I laid the foundation of the earth?" (Job 38:4). By reciting aspects of His authority, wisdom, and power, God forces the murmuring Job to acknowledge his littleness (Job 42:1-6).

But Job might be considered a relatively minor case of personal revolt, if it is indeed proper to speak in such terms, for in another place Paul seems to have encountered a much more hardened version of the same. In Romans, the apostle highlights the prerogatives of the Creator, describing God as One who is free to do what He pleases. In the final analysis, "He has mercy on whom He desires, and He hardens whom He desires" (Romans 9:18).

This pronouncement of God's prerogatives is typically met with protest, and the objection is predictable. If God has indeed planned all that there is or will be, how can human beings be held accountable? As the passage reads: "Who resists His will" (19)? On the surface this reaction appears quite reasonable, and many devout believers have sought answers to these very questions.

Still, Paul detects an attitude of mutiny on the part of some. There are those who are not truly interested in issues of philosophical or theological truth but rather use this teaching of divine sovereignty as an excuse for dodging culpability. With such an audience, Paul is very candid. He asks, "The thing molded will not say to the molder, 'Why did you make me like this,' will it" (20)? God, in other words, is not obliged to provide answers to the inquiries of those who spurn His name. Paul's plan, therefore, takes the form of counter-attack, reminding his readers that, whatever their obstinacy, God is still God.

In the real world, it can be very difficult, if not impossible, to determine the true attitude of a person. While God can read hearts, we clearly cannot (Jeremiah 17:9). Furthermore, all people reflect a mixture of cognitive states, some helpful and some harmful. Thus, identifying rebellion in ourselves or in others is no easy task. The point here is not to get into a blame game but to recognize the truth of divine Lordship. Whatever any of us might think, the Bible plainly teaches that we will one day give an account of ourselves to God (1 Corinthians 3:10-13).

2. The Intellectual: An Inquisitive Mind

Of course not all fit into the category of rebel. There are those with no deep-seeded hostility who simply have unresolved intellectual difficulties. For such, the problem of evil is not an excuse for impiety. Instead, it is an opportunity to ask tough questions, hoping to reach reasonable solutions. These are thinkers.[13] While no one can claim complete sincerity of motive, and though all of us are guilty of suppressing aspects of the truth, these investigators are at least curious and potentially open to discovery.

When it comes to the thinker, simplistic answers will not suffice. What they need (in part, if not primarily) is intellectual support, that is, an honest and firm basis for belief. This can be provided in a variety of ways. For instance it might be feasible to point out the Bible's veracity. Or, a survey of predictive prophecy might be helpful, or a review of redemptive history, in which the attractiveness of truth is a powerful apologetic. As to the subject of evil, these individuals require the employment of deeper philosophical and/or theological arguments.[14]

---

[13]The thinking referred to here is certainly not limited to scholarly endeavors and the realms of higher education. What is in view is simply any person who asks questions and seeks answers.

[14]A sampling of helpful resources might include the following: C. Stephen Evans, *Why Believe? - Reasons and Mystery as Pointers to God* (Grand Rapids, MI: William B. Eerdmans Publishing Company, 1996), John G. Stackhouse, Jr., *Can God Be Trusted?: Faith and the Challenge of Evil* (New York, NY: Oxford University Press, 1998), John Warwick Montgomery, ed., *Evidence for Faith: Deciding the God Question* (Dallas, TX: Probe Books, 1991), Robert C. Newman, ed., *The Evidence of Prophecy*, Hatfield, PA: Interdisciplinary Biblical Research Institute, 1994), R. Douglas Geivett and Gary R. Habermas, eds., *In*

Hints of a certain type of apologetic argumentation are numerous. The book of Lamentations deals with human suffering, as does the story of Job. Then, there is the apostle Paul who points out that human evil is a consequence of unbelief, a rejection of the Creator's ways (Romans 1:18ff). In other places God's inscrutable plan is in view (Romans 9:6-11).

Though the specifics will vary, the important thing to remember is that some people have genuine intellectual struggles, which must be met with intellectual acumen. The biblical writers provide a basis for addressing these matters.

3. The Grieving: A Wounded Soul

A third category of complaint amid suffering is well-represented by the early Thessalonian Christians. These believers were understandably hurt when some among their number had died. Their hurt was compounded, however, because of a misunderstanding concerning Jesus' return. For some reason they thought the status of those who died prior to this event had been compromised, resulting in a forfeiture of blessings associated with the Parousia.[15]

Paul corrected this error by explaining that those who have died in Christ will not miss out on these blessings. In fact they will be the first to be raised from the grave (1 Thessalonians 4:16). At that time, all believers will be reunited with their Lord. Because this is so, there is comfort to be found, even in the midst of death (4:18).

When it comes to enduring human suffering, this scene from Thessalonica is very informative. Here is a group of believers who are extremely grieved by the death of their loved ones. Not only have they lost their friends, but important and comforting truths have been neglected. Those who remained had forgotten (or had never grasped) that Christian grief is not without hope. Paul draws attention to this fact, showing that,

---

Defense of Miracles: A Comprehensive Case for God's Action in History (Downers Grove, IL: InterVarsity Press, 1997), For more information see the bibliography.
[15]Parousia, which means "coming" or "presence," is a term associated with the return of Jesus to planet earth.

hurt as they might be, their sadness must be balanced by thoughts of the great future awaiting those who trust in Jesus (see Chapter 8).

This particular group, the wounded, is not stumped by intellectual riddles but rather hurt by circumstances. The problem of evil for them is one of pain and sorrow. A significant part of a Christian theodicy is along these lines, and believers must be prepared to deal with hurting people. Though this example is of grieving Christians, the general principles outlined here are applicable to all people who suffer. While some seek deeper solutions to these dilemmas, many require only a listening ear and a shoulder on which to cry. Simple prayer, heartfelt concern, a recounting of God's promises, and reminders of hope–these are what many need most.

Conclusion

The above-listed categories are surely generalizations, admitting a wide range of variance. In fact most people fit (at one time or another, if not simultaneously) into more than one of these groups. What is significant for our purposes is that there is more than a single response to human suffering.

Given that no two situations are exactly alike, we are all in need of much discernment. Our prayer, therefore, must be that God Himself would supply wisdom (James 3:13-17), enabling us, both personally and in relating to others, to respond appropriately to the pain, suffering, and evil that so dominates our current existence.

Excursus:

When Skeptics Ask

The only way that believers will be able to meet doubters and agnostics where they are is if they (the doubters and skeptics) are taken seriously. Unfortunately, however, some Christians are all too prone to minimize the legitimacy of questions posed by those who are struggling with or even denying faith. This is due, in part, to an overly skeptical opinion among believers of natural man's abilities and intentions. Thus, so the argument goes, the uncertainty or antagonism of non-Christians is mostly a result of their rebellion against God.

On the one hand, it is certainly understandable that Christians would question the motives of those who are often described in less than flattering terms. On the other hand, some kind of balance is required, for although there are indeed descriptions in Scripture of those who are spiritually biased against the things of God (see Romans 3:9ff; 1 Corinthians 2:14), these same individuals are also divine-image bearers (see Genesis 1:26-27; Jams 3:9).

The image of God is a rich and fascinating concept, pointing to a number of relevant ideas. For one, the divine image—to the degree that it surfaces in fallen man—yields much information about the Maker; the creative power, ingenuity, and genius of the divine-image Giver are

21

evident, at some level, in His creatures. Second, the divine imprint in all human beings provides a genuine point of contact with those who do not currently follow Jesus. Concomitantly, it should cause believers to realize the potential legitimacy of non-Christian objections and questions, and to take these seriously.

I have witnessed on too many occasions how quickly some Christians offer supposedly "tried and true" answers to objections, only to underestimate the complexity of the issue at hand. Amazingly, some Christians fail to recognize the foolishness that remains in their own hearts; having received forgiveness and other immense blessings does not guarantee that we are significantly wiser than our non-Christian counterparts. Indeed, in our criticisms of others, it is all too easy to be condescending and arrogant, traits that belie our true status as humble recipients of grace. Thus, while certain doubters do indeed exude an arrogant spirit, this does not excuse the overly simplistic and, frankly, shoddy efforts of certain defenders of the faith.

Many people, including those outside of the faith, are quite capable of genuine intellectual reflection. In fact they are sometimes more able to get to the heart of a matter because they lack the natural defensiveness of some Christians, especially among those who feel they must have all of the answers. The thing to remember in dealing with those outside of the faith is the need to strike a right balance. Though unbelief and skepticism are often the outworking of impure motives, many of the questions of skeptics are quite legitimate. To the degree that this is the case, we must humbly respect their inquiries.

"Reason's last step is the recognition that there are an infinite number of things which are beyond it."

Blaise Pascal

Chapter 4

Partial (Yet Incomplete) Explanations for Evil

Human tragedy is a numbing thing, draining the vitality from life. But suffering can also be a motivator, for it causes those held in its clutches to ask, "Why?" Of course it is easier to pose a question than to answer it. And even when people are satisfied with their conclusions, this does not guarantee that our solutions are correct.

This is especially true when it comes to the problem of evil. Christians so badly want to receive comfort and so desperately want to clear God of any charges of blame that they can tend to give undue weight to inadequate or incomplete explanations for the presence of evil. When this happens, however, other portions of a sound theodicy are missed or minimized, and a large number of individuals, some believers and some not, are understandably frustrated by overly simplistic responses.

Our next task, therefore, will be to review a number of the incomplete and, in some cases, faulty attempts at theodicy that have been proposed by theologians, philosophers, and others. While some of these efforts do indeed play a role in constructing a well-orbed theodicy, none of them yields a completely satisfactory explanation for evil in a good God's world.

1. The Greater-Good Defense

This view has some merit (see below, 38-40), for there are indeed times when God appears to allow certain evil events to transpire in order to accomplish some good that might not otherwise occur. For instance, though the entrance of sin into the world was a horrible thing, it did allow God the opportunity to become a merciful Rescuer.

Still, though no one doubts that God may indeed produce marvelous things through awful means, it is difficult to see how God Himself avoids implication in the evil He uses in accomplishing His purposes. *That* God is innocent is a biblical axiom; *how* this is so is not easily ascertained. Though this type of theodicy provides some answers, the answers are only partial. The "greater-good" view can only go so far in supplying a useful defense.

2. The Best-Possible World

This resembles the above view, but it posits even more. Not only does God bring about good through evil, but this world (our world) is actually optimal. God did not need to create. Having done so, however, His purpose requires precisely what we observe in the world.

Such a theodicy is liable to the same objection noted in the "greater-good" defense. Furthermore, though evil can be used as an instrument for good, it is difficult to understand why so much evil would be required. Might not God have accomplished the same goals without allowing for such a huge proportion of human tragedy and suffering?

Whatever good is wrought through evil circumstances, it does not follow that God could not have made a better world. Though His wisdom is not to be questioned, it is also imperative that we do not place limitations on what He might have accomplished in some other hypothetical world. Indeed, even if this were the best possible world, i.e., best from the perspective of the entire process and eventual culmination of redemptive history, this "best" world still contains much evil that is not easily explained.[16]

---

[16]See John Frame's discussion in *Apologetics to the Glory of God*, 157-159.

3. Certain Versions of the Free-Will Theodicy

Some proponents of free-will posit that in order to create responsible beings God endowed humans with a type of freedom that is substantially independent of divine constraint. Says Basinger:

> [Since] God has chosen to create a world in which we possess significant freedom, and since we can be significantly free only if he does not unilaterally control how this freedom is utilized, God voluntarily forfeits control over earthly affairs in those cases where he allows us to exercise that freedom.[17]

Thus, so the argument goes, evil is the free choice of rational creatures, with God playing a minimal role in human decisions. Humans make foolish choices, for which God cannot be held accountable.

Clearly, there is a real sense in which men are free moral agents. Indeed, certain advocates of divine sovereignty seem to have missed this point, failing to recognize the significance and the complexity of these issues. But, however free-will is defined, both the amount of freedom assumed by certain free-will advocates and the sufficiency of the free-will defense seem overstated. Indeed, the Scriptures everywhere affirm that, whatever freedom man possesses, he is unable, apart from divine assistance, to know God personally. "This inability to believe is moral, not metaphysical; but it is real inability nonetheless."[18] Far from unhindered autonomy, mankind's inclination is to make wrong choices. The things

---

[17]David Basinger, "Practical Implications" in *The Openness of God: A Biblical Challenge to the Traditional Understanding of God* (Downers Grove: InterVarsity Press, 1994), 159. Certain portions of this volume are a refreshing challenge to an imbalanced view of the interplay between divine sovereignty and human responsibility. There are indeed some who so emphasize God's control that human freedom is all but eliminated. On the other hand, the problem with some of the *Openness* formulations is that they do practically the same thing in the opposite direction, redefining (or ignoring) the meaning of the sovereignty passages in order to defend human freedom. Indeed, whatever "gain" the openness view provides, the loss is substantial. A better way to approach these matters is to hold both strands of the data in tension (see chapter 7). Cf. D. A. Carson, *Divine Sovereignty and Human Responsibility: Biblical Perspectives in Tension* (Grand Rapids, MI: Baker Books, 1981), esp. 201-222.

[18]Carson, *Divine Sovereignty and Human Responsibility*, 165.

that matter most are "foolishness to him; and he cannot understand them" (1 Corinthians 2:14).[19] At some level, therefore, man's freedom is limited by his own nature.

Furthermore, even the free choices of man fall under God's sway. Though, on the one hand, God never tempts a person to perform evil (James 1:13ff), it is still true, on the other hand, that even evil falls under the umbrella of divine sovereignty. As God declares through Isaiah (45:6-7):

> That men may know from the rising to the setting of the sun, That there is no one besides Me. I am the LORD, and there is no other, The One forming light and creating darkness, Causing well-being and creating calamity; I am the LORD who does all these.

At this level, the problem of evil reappears, and the free-will defense, however helpful at certain points, proves incomplete.

Some formulations of free-will better fit the biblical data and are useful in creating a theodicy. Still, evangelicals often disagree on the exact manner in which freedom is to be defined, and they have historically believed that, however one understands freedom, God still reigns in human affairs. Thus, it is difficult to see how any version of free-will, however biblical, can eliminate the tension. As Blocher notes: "It is salutary to emphasize that evil has its origin in freedom; but every theory which magnifies that truth until it becomes an explanation and a solution to the problem is just a conjuring trick."[20]

In one sense man's "freedom" renders him culpable, and this is surely a piece of a well-constructed apologetic (see chapter 7). In another sense, however, this does not in itself solve the problem of evil.

---

[19]Recognizing the problem of spiritual blindness in man, some have proposed that it is Adam in particular who is to be blamed for evil. He, after all, possessed significantly more freedom than his progeny. But, if God in some way permitted the fall of the first man, as orthodox thinkers maintain, the problem remains.

[20]Blocher, *Evil and the Cross*, 64.

4. The Limited (or Self-Limiting) Deity

This concept, which is sometimes related to the previous view, can take on a number of different twists. There are some, like Harold Kushner, who, given the current state of this world, cannot bring themselves to accept that God is both all-powerful and all-loving. Kushner, feeling that he must reject one of these beliefs, decides that it is easier to jettison the omnipotence of God. Others, such as Clark Pinnock, envision that, in order to allow for human autonomy, God placed certain limitations on what He would allow Himself to know.

For the Christian theist, the difficulty with these and similar views is that they do not square with Scripture, where God is portrayed as knowing and directing all things.[21] In fact it is hard to imagine what comfort can be found in a divine being whose attributes are minimized or eliminated. Responding to the implications of a watered down deity, Carson writes: "To abandon belief in the omnipotence of God may 'solve' the problem of evil, but the cost is enormous: the resulting god is incapable of helping us—not now, and not in the future."[22]

None of this denies that there is a sense in which God places "limitations" on Himself in redeeming fallen man. Philippians 2:5-8, one of the key passages concerning the incarnation, may hint at such an idea. There, we are told that Jesus "emptied Himself, taking the form of a bond-servant."[23] Furthermore, there is little doubt that God must accommodate Himself to His creatures in order to create, relate to, and redeem them. Still, regarding the presence of evil, it is self-defeating to formulate a position that answers certain difficulties while creating greater ones.

---

[21] God's omniscience is found in numerous passages, including Psalm 139, Isaiah 46:10, and Hebrews 4:11-13. Among the omnipotence passages are the following: Psalm 115:3; Isaiah 14:24; 55:11; Luke 18:27. God's sovereignty is highlighted in such places as Romans 11:33-36 and 1 Timothy 6:15-16.

[22] D. A. Carson, *How Long, O Lord?-Reflections on Suffering and Evil* (Grand Rapids, MI: Baker Books, 1990), 31.

[23] See Gordon D. Fee, *Paul's Letter to the Philippians* (Grand Rapids, MI: William B. Eerdmans Publishing Company), 197-214 and Peter T. O'Brien, *The Epistle to the Philippians* (Grand Rapids, MI: William B. Eerdmans Publishing Company, 1991), 186-232.

5. Evil as an Illusion

One sure way of avoiding the problem of evil is by denying its very existence. Certain eastern religions hold to this position, as do some cults. One wonders, however, how something that is not real can cause so much heartache. If evil is an illusion, everything else might also be, including the attempt to label it as such. Says Frame:

> There is no reason to say that evil is an illusion. Further, to say that it is, is to play games with words. For if evil is an illusion, it is a terribly troublesome illusion, an illusion that brings misery, pain, suffering, and death. If it is said that the pain also is illusory, I reply that there is no difference between illusory pain and real pain so far as the problem of evil is concerned. The problem just backs up a step and asks: "How could a good God give us all such a terrible illusion of pain?" One great advantage of Scripture's viewpoint is that it doesn't play games with suffering people. In Scripture, evil is treated quite simply as something we must deal with, whatever its metaphysical status may be.[24]

Categorizing suffering as an illusion, therefore, is no real answer to the problem. Indeed, the pervasiveness and intensity of evil are such that no serious theodicy that denies its existence can expect to calm the hearts and feed the minds of those who encounter it each day.

6. God as ex Lex (i.e., Outside of the Law)

This view, proposed for instance by Gordon Clark, says that God is a law unto Himself, and that He can do whatever He wants.[25] Since He transcend His creatures, He is not subject to the same "rules" as they are.

Some of this is quite accurate, for the living God has prerogatives that humans lack. In general, however, the Bible's moral code is a reflection of the One who gave it. Therefore, "[we] can be assured that God will behave

---

[24]Frame, *Apologetics to the Glory of God*, 156.
[25]Gordon Clark, *Religion, Reason, and Revelation* (Philadelphia: Presbyterian & Reformed Publishing Company, 1961).

according to the same standards of holiness that he prescribes for us, except insofar as Scripture declares a difference between his responsibilities and ours. But on this basis, the problem of evil returns."[26]

In other words we do not normally expect God to arbitrarily violate the very principles that He Himself has provided. For instance, when God commands us to tell the truth, we assume that He can be counted on to do the same (Titus 1:2). Though God's perspective transcends our own, and while the appearance of impropriety on God's part is just that, an *appearance*, this does not solve our dilemma. Indeed, this is precisely why evil is considered a problem. Though God *is* innocent of any charges, we find it difficult, if not impossible, to determine *how* this can be the case. Again, however helpful this category might appear, the problem of evil persists.

7. The Indirect-Cause View

Some theorize that the way God avoids blame for evil is through the avenue of secondary causes. "The argument seems to be that since God is the indirect rather than the direct cause of evil, he bears no blame for it."[27]

There is no doubt some truth to this idea. God does stand behind evil in an "indirect" fashion. Thus, He distances Himself from what James (1:13ff) calls "tempting" someone to evil.[28] Still, one would be hard pressed to accept this theory as a completely satisfactory explanation for evil. Frame's evaluation is to the point:

> Indirectness of causality does not in itself mitigate responsibility–at least on the human level. If I hire a hit man to kill someone, I am as responsible for the murder as the man who pulls the trigger. Scripture warns us that enticing someone else to sin is itself a sin (Deut. 13:6ff; Rom. 14). Is God so different from creatures in this respect that the indirectness of his role in evil insulates him against moral censure? Scripture never says that he is different in that way.[29]

---

[26]Frame, *Apologetics to the Glory of God*, 68.

[27]Ibid., 165.

[28]See Douglas J. Moo, *James* (Grand Rapids: InterVarsity Press, 1997), 70ff.

[29]Frame, *Apologetics to the Glory of God*, 166. In answer to Frame's question, there is of course a sense in which the answer is "yes." That is, God is obviously in some ways

As helpful as this response may be at one level, at another (deeper?) level it fails to provide any ultimate answers, and so the problem remains.

8. The Ad Hominem Response

There are some who deny the need for a theodicy in the first place, claiming, for a variety of reasons, that evil is no problem at all. Thus, when a theologian, philosopher, or common person inquires as to God's involvement in human suffering, the question itself is considered improper, and the inquirer is denounced as a compromiser. This is an *ad hominem* response in which an attack is made on the inquirer's character or motives while his actual questions or disagreements are never really addressed.

That certain inquiries are arrogant and inappropriate is clear enough. In such scenarios the human questioner may need to be confronted about his attitude (see 15-17). But this does not mean that all questioning, even when arising from mixed motives, is illegitimate. It would seem more honest and helpful to acknowledge our ignorance and lack of information than to launch an assault on those looking for solutions to admittedly difficult issues.

No Christian theodicy should be so pessimistic as to leave people without a solid hope, a hope that is reasonable and substantial. Then again, there is no comprehensive solution to many of the troublesome issues of life. Consequently, those who pose hard questions are not to be dismissed.

9. Evil as Temporary

A rather fascinating response to evil and suffering is that, given the promise of eternity, we only suffer for a relatively short period of time. This mind-set is in view, for instance, when the apostle Paul, who had endured much persecution, depicts his travails as "momentary, light affliction" (2 Corinthians 4:17). From the perspective of eternity, the trouble we encounter in this life will seem like "a flash in the pan."

---

bafflingly different from us. These differences, whatever they are, plunge us deeper into mystery, even as they force us to continue pondering additional explanations for evil.

This argument makes some sense, for a billion years from now (if we can, indeed, speak of eternity in terms of years) the experiences we had in this life will pale in comparison to the realities before us. Indeed, the beatific vision, the immediate presence of God, along with the vantage point afforded those living in a glorified state, will surely give new perspective to the heartache we encountered during our sojourn on earth.

Of course this is yet another example of why evil is currently such a problem. While we can imagine in some small way that a lifetime of heartache will be overshadowed by an eternity of bliss, we are not now in a place to experience this blessed outlook. Though we can and should seek to live in accordance with this hope, we are still stuck, at this time, in the here-and-now of human ignorance, sin, and pain. Furthermore, even though evil will eventually leave us, there are still intellectual puzzles to consider. While the duration of evil is limited, it is evil none-the-less. Even if the problem is minimized from the vantage point of eternity, it does not go away entirely. We must take what we can from this perspective, even as we acknowledge that many of our questions remain unanswered.

Conclusion

To this list might be added a number of other (sometimes different, sometimes overlapping) explanations for evil. For example there is the so-called soul-making theodicy of John Hick and others (that in some ways resembles the "greater-good" response mentioned above); this proposes that suffering is required in order for the soul to be nurtured and brought to maturity. Others opt for a variety of solutions in which human autonomy is highlighted. Still others place evil within some type of evolutionary grid. In all of these options, nothing close to a complete solution to the problem of evil is to be found, and certain proposals create more problems than they solve.

While some of the above explanations offer a ray of hope, there remains no single solution to the problem of evil. Given the complexities of God and His world, perhaps this would be an unrealistic expectation. At the least, however, we have considered some options, which might assist us as we seek more clues to this riddle.

*"Pieces of the puzzle make funny shapes,
but they all fit together in the end."*

Mr. Flippers, *Hoodwinked*

Chapter 5

Pieces of the Puzzle:
Seeking a Biblical Perspective on Evil

Constructing a theodicy is a messy project, defying simplistic solutions. Indeed, there appears to be no single, unifying explanation for this dark reality. It is probably best, therefore, to view the problem of evil as a kind of theological and philosophical puzzle, a puzzle in which God has provided an assortment of pieces.

Because of the complexity of the subject, the approach taken here will be multifaceted. Drawing on some of the ideas already mentioned, and adding a number of other concepts, the goal is to provide a broad framework for constructing a Christian theodicy. By considering various factors that shed light on this great theoretical and personal mystery, I hope that the reader will be fortified in the faith and enabled to better cope with the inequities of life. What follows are some perspectives on the problem of evil.

1. Evil is the expected outworking of life in a fallen world.

In view of the Bible's claims, it is no surprise that evil dominates this world. From cover to cover, the authors of Scripture depict this planet as cursed or, as theologians have described it, fallen. Humanity's first parents rebelled against their Maker (Genesis 3:1ff) and ever since, life has been hard and often tragic. Though suffering represents a dreadful problem for all people, there is a sense in which the presence of evil actually confirms a biblical worldview. In contrast with certain attempts to portray life as perpetually happy and carefree, the real world is sometimes filled with brutality and pain. The Bible predicted (or at least allowed for) such a scenario many centuries ago. Obviously, this does not answer all of the questions surrounding the enigma of evil. It does, however, provide some perspective, reminding us that we live in the type of world described in the Bible.

2. Often (though not always) evil is the result of foolish choices.

In an immensely sobering passage, the book of Romans records that those who persist in impiety create a situation in which they can be "given over" to their proclivities (Romans 1:2, 26, 28), what Scripture sometimes terms *sin*. Sin, of course, is evil. Yet here we see this evil as the penalty for human corruption. Man chooses to perform evil and receives it back on himself. In this context, amazingly, it is even equated with the wrath of God. Judgment sometimes comes when those who persist in wrongful choices are enslaved by those choices–a frightening thought indeed, and one explanation for the evil that abounds.

It is important to note, therefore, that much (not all) tragedy is integrally connected to faulty and unwise decisions. On such occasions the evil that ensues is due primarily to human foolishness. Far from implicating God in evil, numerous cases might be provided in which humanity is the responsible party. As Anselm wrote: "You have not yet duly estimated the gravity of sin."

3. Sometimes, evil's occurrence leads to something good.

In Hebrews 12:4ff, the author informs his readers that God disciplines his children for their good. Part of this discipline involves rubbing shoulders with that which is evil; God, in other words, can use evil to perfect His children. Think, for instance, of the example of Joseph, who was abandoned by his family and left for dead (Genesis 45:1; 50:15-20). All appeared lost until years later when Joseph was finally able to turn to his brothers and declare, "You meant evil against me, but God meant it for good" (Genesis 50:20). It is not that evil itself is good, of course, but that God brings about good by way of human depravity (Romans 8:28).

Even more astounding is the fact that Christ Himself "learned obedience from the things which He suffered" (Hebrews 5:8), much of which entailed contact with corrupt people and their evil schemes. Indeed, the most heinous act of history, the crucifixion of God's Son, became the path by which the most incredible work of grace was made available. Through the absolute worst, God accomplished the absolute best (Acts 2:22-24; 3:13ff).

None of this is intended to imply that all evil necessarily yields a greater good, and even when good things result, it is important to recognize that not all of these are immediately observable. However, at least some evil is used by God to (eventually) create greater blessings. Though there are other possible explanations, and while this does not exhaustively answer our questions, it does provide one aspect of a biblically informed theodicy.

Through suffering, endurance has been increased, rebellion stymied, character molded, and love magnified. Though the reasons why God has chosen to do things this way and to operate through so many horrific circumstances is not hereby understood, it is nonetheless true that in the world God created, suffering can sometimes lead to surprising benefits.

4. The existence of evil enables God to display aspects of his character that would otherwise remain hidden.

As previously mentioned, God permits evil in order to put His justice and power on display (Romans 9:22) and to make known the riches of His glory (9:23). To put it bluntly, the existence of evil affords God the opportunity to show forth aspects of His character (some quite fearful) that might otherwise remain hidden. What's more, He accomplishes a depth of mercy, a height of grace, and breadth of wisdom that stand in stark contrast to what human beings deserve. God thus allows evil to be the dark backdrop upon which He paints His magnificent portraits of grace.

In Ephesians 3:9-10 history is seen as a stage upon which God vindicates Himself before the angelic hosts. The human story, in other words, is really *His* story. As the Writer and Director of the human play, God has seen fit to, as it were, display His wares. Two of the most striking examples of this are His justice and His love. In order for these facets of His being to be recognized, the divine script had to include bad characters and evil plots.[30] Thus, "evil ultimately serves a good purpose. Its existence makes it possible for God to demonstrate to all the universe what He is like."[31] As an amplification of the previous point, we see here that the presence of evil, though surely baffling, provides God a platform for demonstrating His divine qualities.

5. At some level, the existence of evil is (and, perhaps, always will be) a mystery.

The Church does itself little service when it trivializes the hard questions of life (see 32). Evil is a reality that deeply affects the lives of countless people. And when suffering occurs, a number of completely understandable and often legitimate questions come to the fore. These, of course, concern God's involvements in human pain and the like.

---

[30]The point here is not that God was compelled to allow evil. Evil is necessary only in the sense that certain choices of God are contingent upon the type of world in which He operates. Grace does not have to be expressed. But if God chooses to be gracious, He must (apparently) create a world in which grace is required. Both retribution and mercy, in order to be demonstrated, require the presence of evil. As noted above, however, this does not necessarily imply a "best-possible-world" scenario. One might imagine a world in which other divine traits are given expression, or God might have displayed His love in a world containing significantly less evil. At least from the standpoint of human thought, it is difficult to prove that this world in the best possible. All that is known for sure is that God has chosen to create our world, and He knows what He is doing even when we do not!

[31]Jay Adams, *The Grand Demonstration: A Biblical Study of the So-Called Problem of Evil* (Santa Barbara, CA: EastGate Publishers, 1991), 51. Though Adams tends to come across with a bit too much dogmatism, sometimes treating the problem of evil as if it were a child's puzzle, he is surely correct in describing God as the good and wise Architect of all things.

Clearly, some of the objections of skeptics are not intellectual at all but moral and spiritual; in these cases the problem is not one of understanding but of antagonism toward spiritual things. Still, this does not negate the fact that there are indeed missing pieces to our theodicy. Why God would allow such rampant evil to inflict His children is not always easy to see. Could He not accomplish His purpose in some less severe way? Cannot the all-powerful and all-loving Lord bypass some of the more extreme circumstances in executing His plan? There are, no doubt, good answers to these and similar questions–some which are available now, others which may not be revealed until the eschaton. What is important here is that believers in a good and sovereign God neither minimize evil nor exaggerate their comprehension of how God relates to it. While certain matters can be discerned now, and others can be partially grasped, some things are, frankly, baffling.

Conclusion

Though this categorization is by no means exhaustive, a number of insights can be gleaned from the exercise. First, it is obvious that the objections made against theism generally and against Christianity in particular are not always answerable in an easy and straightforward manner. Human beings, made in the image of their Maker, are much too complex and clever to expect such a simplistic and predictable solution. Second, God Himself is not so easily apprehended. The reasons for His decisions are sometimes hard, if not impossible, to grasp.

Since believers worship a God whose character and record are coherent, there is no need to fret at the prospect of evil. Although countless people have experienced the pangs of living in a fallen world, and while trials have often led them to ask why this is so, it is possible to approach this problem from the perspective of faith.

> The mystery of God and evil in particular looms large on every thoughtful Christian's horizon. But Christians look around and say, even in the presence of such mysteries, that life and the Christian faith correspond well. So they trust God for what they do not yet (and perhaps never will) understand.[32]

---

[32]Stackhouse, *Can God Be Trusted?* 148-149.

The intention here has been to provide a basis for thinking through the problem of evil within a Christian worldview. Though mystery will not go away, and many of God's ways remain hidden, the living God *has* revealed enough of Himself to support us along the way. As we struggle against the many expressions of evil and suffering, the enigmas will remain. But, with the help of God and others, faith will remain, as well.[33] Where we cannot see, we must learn to trust. As Genesis states: "the Judge of all the earth [will] deal justly" (18:25). Amid a whole lot of mystery, there are solid reasons to believe, and there is hope.

---

[33]Though God is sovereign in all affairs, He apparently relates to good and evil in different ways. See Carson, *Divine Sovereignty and Human Responsibility*, 212.

Excursus:

Is it Ever Right to Complain?

It is common, when tragedy strikes, when evil rears its ugly head, to give voice to our pain. The great majority of us have on many occasions given expression to our frustration with the inequities of life. We complain, and our complaints are usually of the personal sort, the questions we ask relating to God's fairness or goodness, or at least His wisdom, in allowing bad things to touch our lives.

To complain is to express dissatisfaction, to acknowledge ignorance, to proclaim hurt. The appropriateness or inappropriateness of the complaint depends on the attitude of the one making it. In one sense, of course, complaining can be a very arrogant and irreverent thing to do. Who are we, after all, to sit in judgment over God, seeking, in essence, to dethrone Him? This self-proclaimed autonomy is condemned, for instance, in Romans 9. There we are told in no uncertain terms that such an attitude amounts to rebellion. God, Paul tells us, can do what He wants with His creation. This means that all complaining that attacks the character and denies the prerogatives of the Lord must be avoided. Segments of the church, recognizing this fact, have typically stood against complaining, treating it as unspiritual.

But not all complaining is wrong, for there is a type of complaining that is a part of the human fabric, a proper reaction against pain and evil. "Evening and morning and at noon, I will complain and murmur, And He will hear my voice" (Psalm 55:17). "I pour out my complaint before Him; I declare my trouble before Him" (Psalm 142:2). Many of the Psalms are instances of such legitimate complaints (e.g., 5; 83; 88; 94). Commenting on the contrast that is sometimes seen between the church's attitude toward suffering and that which is advocated in the lament Psalms, Brueggemann says, "At least it is clear that a church that goes on singing 'happy songs' in the face of raw reality is doing something very different from what the Bible itself does."[34] Sometimes, in other words, we are driven more by misinformed religious expectations than we are by the truth itself. When this happens, we are the losers for it.

> What is said to Yahweh may be scandalous and without redeeming social value; but these speakers are completely committed, and whatever must be said about the human situation must be said directly to Yahweh, who is Lord of the human experience and partner with us in it. That does not mean things are toned down. Yahweh does not have protective sensitivities. Yahweh is expected and presumed to receive the fullness of Israel's speech.[35]

What makes the cries of the Psalmist valid is authentic faith. Those who approach God in honest and humble trust are free to bombard heaven with their questions, for these are not ultimately grounded in rebellion or self-centeredness. They arise, rather, from a heart convinced that God is good and His ways are right, even if we cannot detect exactly how this works out in our lives. People in such a condition are invited to express their uneasiness and confusion. When this occurs, the "complainer" is not led astray but actually closer to the One who alone can provide comfort for an aching heart. Therefore, while it is improper and foolish to demand anything close to perfect understanding, it is proper to stretch one's faith through the process of asking why.

---

[34]Walter Brueggemann, *Spirituality of the Psalms* (Minneapolis, MN: Augsburg Fortress Press, 2002), 26.
[35]Ibid., 30.

"To everything (turn, turn, turn)
There is a season (turn, turn, turn)
And a time for every purpose, under heaven."

The Byrds, *Turn, Turn, Turn*
(adapted from Ecclesiastes)

Chapter 6

Job, the Invisible World, and Evil

The affairs of this world are just that, the affairs of *this* world. According to Scripture, however, they are also more, for invisible forces impact what takes place in our lives. Examples of this in Scripture are numerous, but one very pertinent story is that of Job, who encountered horrendous circumstances that were due to forces unseen.

Job was a godly man, and God was pleased with him. Behind the scenes, however, Satan wanted to test Job to see if he was all that God made him out to be. Interestingly, God Himself is the one who draws attention to the righteousness of His servant, eventually granting Satan permission to intervene in Job's life.

Great harm is inflicted by Satan upon Job and his family. Job loses practically everything in a series of tragedies that are practically unparalleled in most people's experience. Still, through it all, Job keeps his faith, determined not to deny God.

Over time, though, Job is understandably weakened and begins to question his circumstances. In response God comes to Job in a whirlwind, providing Job with both a framework of divine authority and a demonstration of His awesome presence. As a result, Job is humbled, God restores him, and we are left with a theodicy for the ages.

Satan's discussions with God, God's granting of permission, Satan's activity–all of these were orchestrated from "offstage." Both Job and his friends were surely aware of the impact of God on human events, but none of them had any real insight into the activity taking place in the spirit realm. As a result, they were all left to guess and, often, to misinterpret what was occurring.

Those who read this story, however, are in a different place, for we are allowed access to many things of which the characters in the story were unaware.

> Indeed, the irony of the story is that we, the readers, are privy to the heavenly conversation between Satan and God that, mysterious as it is, gives us at least some clue as to why Job was cursed. The story gives no indication that righteous Job learns any of this. He certainly hears nothing of it when he asks God for answers.[36]

Though we are never given a complete rationale for all that took place in Job's life, we are given access to at least some clues that can assist us in our theodicy making efforts.

One of the more relevant points is the simple recognition that Job's life was influenced by phenomena of which he had little knowledge. How this takes place is largely hidden from us, but that it does is assumed throughout Scripture. Jesus, for instance, confronted and rescued numerous individuals who were possessed by evil spirits. Indeed, Paul writes in hope that "the manifold wisdom of God might now be made known through the church to the rulers and the authorities in the heavenly places" (Ephesians 3:10). The rulers and authorities are those invisible beings who seem to strain to catch a glimpse of what God is doing in the world, at times even playing a role in the outworking of human affairs. The world, in other words, is the landscape upon which God performs His will, and at least some portion of it is for the purpose of displaying His wisdom to the angelic hosts. Again, that which is invisible has an impact on that which is seen.

Concerning a Christian theodicy, we are once again denied access to complete answers. But we are told that the things that take place in this world, including evil, are partly due to things that take place in the realm

---

[36]Stackhouse, *Can God Be Trusted?* 96.

of the invisible. Hebrews say that "what is seen was not made out of things which are visible" (Hebrews 11:3). Similarly, the things that we see in the world–the choices, the outcomes, and even the evil we encounter–are somehow mysteriously tied to that which we cannot see.

However much we can currently grasp, we are in many ways out of our element, unable to glean much about dimensions that are beyond our immediate access. Followers of Jesus must walk by faith and, at the very least, show some restraint when making judgments about these mystifying matters. Above all, we must look to the greatest invisible force of all, the God who is Spirit (John 4:24), asking for assistance, grace, wisdom, hope, and a true sense of His presence.[37]

---

[37]This chapter is not written to support the speculative views of some, who seem to think there is a demon around every corner. Those whose agenda is to locate and cast out all dark forces seem to miss the fact that here in Job nothing of the kind takes place. Indeed, Job is pretty much "in the dark" most of the way. A better application of Job's story would be to acknowledge that some type of spiritual warfare is indeed taking place, but much of it escapes our ability to provide a "blow by blow" account of it. What we can do, however, is recognize that a good God is indeed orchestrating even those things that make no sense to us. Faith, then, is a more biblical response than an overly wildly imagination.

"I cannot imagine faith apart from mystery. Mystery permeates every particle of the truths I hold so dear."

Ruth A. Tucker

❦

Chapter 7

Compatibilism and Divine Mystery

Introduction

Many of the decisions made in constructing a Christian theodicy are interwoven with one's view of divine sovereignty and how it relates to human choice. People on various sides of the debate are prone to emphasize one aspect of the data or the other. Some highlight the sovereignty texts. Others place greater stress on passages dealing with humanity's ability and responsibility to choose. But in order to be faithful to the whole of Scripture, it is important that we give due weight to both divine superintendence and human culpability.

Of course saying that we ought to be faithful to every aspect of Scripture is no guarantee that we will achieve any measure of success in working through these complex issues. As to the manner in which these components (i.e., the human and the divine) fit together, there are numerous difficulties. Says Carson:

> I frankly doubt that finite human beings can cut this Gordian knot; at least, this finite human being cannot. The sovereignty-responsibility tension is not a problem to be solved; rather it is a framework to be

explored. . . . To explore this tension is to explore the nature of God and his ways with men.[38]

A Form of Compatibilism[39]

Great care must be taken with how this tension is handled. To emphasize divine sovereignty at the expense of human freedom reduces men and women to mere automatons. Then again, to accentuate human freedom to the point that divine sovereignty is ignored grossly misrepresents the biblical data. Since neither of these options will do, it might be helpful to introduce the concept of compatibilism.

> Compatibilism contends that a person can act freely even though that action is determined by God. To the compatibilist, actions are free if the actors do them voluntarily, spontaneously or willingly, without coercion by anything outside of themselves, even though their action may be predictable as an expression of their own desires.[40]

---

[38]Carson, *Divine Sovereignty and Human Responsibility*, 2.

[39]The reason I say a *form* of compatibilism is that I have not always been completely satisfied with some of the definitions provided. Compatibilism states that divine determination and human freedom are compatible, which is the primary point. This being said, human beings never possess absolute freedom, that is, the ability to do anything. Some decisions are, frankly, not possible (e.g., I can't simply decide to be a world class sprinter or a professional baseball player. While I might improve my skills, there are certain built in limitations), and all potential decisions are influenced by a multiplicity of factors (social, physical, psychological, spiritual, etc.). Furthermore, as many theologians and philosophers have pointed out, *in*determinate freedom sounds too much like chaos and arbitrariness. If something is truly arbitrary, then not even God could know and predict the future; this does not bode well with the biblical data. Still, some advocates of compatibilism seem to overly limit the meaning and extent of freedom, reducing it to (supposedly) manageable proportions. Here is how I see it: (1) God is sovereign in that He knows and in some way guides all events. (2) Human beings possess real (though limited) freedom. (3) These two statements (1 and 2) are compatible in such a way that neither of them is compromised. (4) In our efforts to reconcile these statements (1 and 2), we must explore the meaning of such concepts as sovereignty, freedom, libertarianism, hard and soft determinism, monergism, synergism, middle knowledge, and others. (5) Ultimately, we are left with much mystery. *That* divine sovereignty and human freedom are compatible is a biblical and theological maxim; *how* this takes place is largely beyond us.

[40]Terrance Tiessen, *Providence and Prayer: How Does God Work in the World?* (Downers Grove, IL: InterVarsity Press, 2000), 365. Of course we might still wish to "push the

What this means is that divine sovereignty and human responsibility must be understood in such a way that the meaning of neither is used to understate or obscure the meaning of the other. "[So] far as the Bible is concerned, the two propositions are taught and are mutually compatible."[41]

This discussion has a significant bearing on the problem of evil. A compatibilist position places blame on humans for the evil they commit, while simultaneously declaring that even evil does not escape the sway of God's sovereignty. However, recognizing that something is true is not the same as explaining it. Somehow, God's relationship to good and evil is dissimilar. When good occurs, God is the One who gets credit (James 1:17). But, when evil takes place, He is never held morally accountable for it (James 1:12-14). In some inscrutable manner, God relates to good and evil in these divergent ways, thus retaining His Lordship in all circumstances.

All of this is ultimately tied to the type of God portrayed in Scripture. On the one hand, He acts, pleads, and responds; God is personal. On the other hand, He is everywhere described as Lord and King, as the Ruler of creation; God is sovereign.

The impact this has on our study is profound, for it indicates that God's permission of evil is somehow related to the complexity of His person. "The mystery of providence is in the first instance not located in debates about free will, the place of Satan, and the like. It is located in the doctrine of God."[42] The enigma of evil, in other words, leads us into the mystery of the Godhead itself. One of the main reasons why we are unable to unravel and make sense of God's providential acts is precisely because we are incapable of fully comprehending Him.

---

envelope," inquiring into the causes of these personal desires. If these are, in part, the result of various social/environmental forces, and if God is ultimately sovereign over such social/environmental conditions, how does this affect our conception of freedom? While Tiessen's appraisal is accurate, it is important to recognize that compatibilism does not eliminate mystery so much as it helps frame these issues in a way that is at least consistent with Scripture's portrayal.

[41]Carson, *How Long, O Lord?* 201. Note his treatment throughout this section (199-227).

[42]Ibid., 218.

Knowing and Not Knowing

Mankind has been endowed with the ability to think, to reason, to interpret God's creation. This is why Paul can state so confidently, "that which is known about God is evident within them; for God made it known to them" (Romans 1:19). We are born with an intuitive awareness that God is, and that He is great (Romans 1:20).

Humanity, however, has often rejected God and His ways. The proneness in man to seek utter independence, that is, a life in which self, not God, is central, has given rise to a twisted outlook (Romans 1:18-23). This is not to deny man's intellectual abilities, which are a gift from God; rather, these God-given faculties are damaged in such a way as to be misused. Though capable of profound insights and impressive acts, humanity is separated from the life of its Creator.

But God has not left man to himself. Divine love and mercy are injected into the life of man, as the Lord Himself comes to the rescue. Amazingly, God's own Son became one of us in order to rescue us from our foolishness and its consequences. As a result, God can be known.

Those who embrace God gradually come to take on a new perspective. Through the Christian Scriptures, God's inscribed Word, there is much to learn about the Savior. God, who is a talking God, has revealed much about Himself and His world so that we might know and live for Him.

It does not take long, however, to realize that God has not revealed everything. Though He has scattered evidences of His power and majesty across the landscape of this world, there remains much that is not known.

Looking at the big picture, these two thoughts emerge: On the one hand, the true God, the God of Scripture, has displayed His glory in conspicuous ways. On the other hand, there are many things He has not revealed to us. One of the unrevealed things is a completely satisfactory explanation for evil.

Whatever might be said about evil, this way of doing things, i.e., of revealing and concealing His ways, is truly extraordinary (even necessary?). If we knew little or nothing about God, faith would amount to an irrational leap in the dark. Then again, if God could be easily grasped, our knowledge of Him would hardly inspire worship.

In contrast with humanly contrived versions of deity, the real God is both a Revealer and a Concealer. He has disclosed enough of Himself to make belief in Him not only rational but compelling. But because many of His ways transcend human comprehension, there is a lot about Him that eludes us.

These two factors (i.e., revelation and mystery) belong together. The fact that God has clearly shown Himself to be reliable and self-consistent indicates that mystery is not to be equated with illogic. Likewise, the acknowledgment of divine mystery is a safeguard against the all-too-common assumption that we pretty much have God figured out.

Our inability to penetrate the enigma of evil is not due to a slip up in the divine plan but is an outworking or implication of God's transcendence. God is far greater than any creature has conceived. If this is so, our next quest must be to determine the proper response to such mystery.

Learning from Mystery

In many circles mystery is treated like a kind of providential error. Something defies explanation and is quickly and almost embarrassingly relegated to this category, hidden away somewhere out of sight. But nothing that we encounter is truly the result of a mistake on God's part, a kind of Plan B. Rather, all things, including the mysteries, are intended to influence our perception of our Maker.

God has not only revealed things about Himself that are easy to grasp, but He has consistently shown that there is much about Him that defies the best of human ingenuity. What this says to us is that God intends for us to notice that He far exceeds our ability to comprehensively understand Him. This is even true when our thoughts of Him, those formulated through careful consideration of what He has clearly revealed, are accurate.

To illustrate, we might say that the Lord is a lot more like an ocean than a pond. Ponds are relatively simple to measure and traverse, for we can locate their edges. Oceans, on the other hand, are not so easily grasped, for their borders are nowhere in sight. Those who stare out at the ocean or, better yet, dive into it, are compelled to acknowledge their littleness. Similarly, when we come to recognize the immensity of our Creator, the ramifications are profound. Among others, the two primary responses are faith and worship.

Though humans are recipients of perspicuous truth from God, not everything is equally clear. While faith is sometimes a matter of embracing clearly defined truth, at times it involves resting in the One whose ways are hard to envision. In either case, we must trust. The God who reveals Himself in the daylight must be trusted in the dark. Mystery, especially the mystery of evil, challenges us to believe in that which is not yet (fully) seen.

Where genuine faith is present, there is also worship, which is greatly enhanced through a proper acceptance of mystery. When we come to accept that God really does possess answers to the most unsolvable human predicaments, the mind boggles. *How* God can make sense of the paradoxes often remains unexplained, but once we accept *that* He can, a new kind of appreciation begins to grow. One can barely imagine how great and wise such a deity must be. White's words are apropos:

> While we may struggle with God's mystery, we are also drawn to it. Our motivation to seek God flows from love coupled with a deep sense of awe; the awe is natural, indispensable. Consider what faith would be like without it. As doubt can lead to faith, mystery can—and should—lead to awe.[43]

There *is* a proper response to the problem of evil. Though evil is bewildering to man, it is not so with the One known as "I Am" (Exodus 3:14; John 8:58). In the end no one will be able to accuse Him of wrong, and all will eventually see enough to realize that He is a good and wise God. As we come to absorb at least some small portion of this now, our faith is fortified.

---

[43]James Emery White, *Embracing the Mysterious God: Loving the God We Don't Understand* (Downers Grove, IL: InterVarsity Press, 2003), 108-109.

"So often times it happens that we live our lives in chains
And we never even know we have the key."

The Eagles, *Already Gone*

Chapter 8

Jesus–Theodicy and Hope

Scripture is filled with moral and spiritual counsel, all of which is intended to equip us in our quest to live successfully before God and men (2 Peter 1:3). But at its core, a biblical worldview is much more than a list of good ideas. It is about a person, the Son of God, Jesus of Nazareth (Colossians 2:2-3, 6ff).

Ephesians speaks of "the summing up of all things in Christ, things in the heavens and things on the earth" (1:10), and Colossians brags that Jesus possesses "all the treasures of wisdom and knowledge" (2:3). As the author of Hebrews puts it: "He is the radiance of [God's] glory and the exact representation of His nature" (1:3). The Old Testament Scriptures anticipate Him (Isaiah 53), and the New Testament announces Him (Mark 1:1). Indeed, the future enjoyment of God's people will find its source in Him (Revelation 21:22).

If these statements are accurate, the subject pursued here, the problem of evil, would best be considered from a Christological perspective, that is, from a vantage point of faith in Jesus. Given His centrality in Christian theology, Jesus must play a major role in any effort to construct a theodicy. This can be fleshed out in a number of ways, all of which demand a closer look at God's unique Son.

First of all, Jesus is like all men—with the obvious exception of having never violated God's commands—having experienced the full gamut of human thoughts and emotions, from immense joy to incomprehensible sorrow. "He had to be made like His brethren in all things, so that He might become a merciful and faithful high priest" (Hebrews 2:17). When it comes to suffering, Jesus has been there.

What's more, Jesus is even able to share in human tragedy now. Though He will not reappear physically until the second advent, this does not restrict His ministry. Indeed, He promised the disciples that He would not forsake them but would come to them in the person of His Spirit (John 14:16-19). It can be said, therefore, that Jesus has suffered *like* humanity (during his earthly ministry) and, in some strange mystical way, does suffer *with* humanity (through the Spirit today). But there is more, for God's Son has also suffered *for* humanity, taking to Himself the full gamut of human iniquity. Jesus "who knew no sin" was constituted sin and so treated like a sinner (2 Corinthians 5:21). The Holy One was treated (by His father, and for our sake!) as if He were unholy.

In an utterly striking display of humility, the Son of God entered this suffering world. At Jesus birth, throughout His life, and finally in His ignominious death, there is a constant conflict with evil. It pursued Him from His mother's womb (Matthew 2:16ff), confronted Him in the desert (Matthew 4:1ff), and sought to corner Him on countless occasions. Eventually, evil lead to His betrayal (Matthew 26:14ff), gave Him over to a crowd whose battle cry was "Crucify Him!" (Matthew 27:22), and escorted Him to Golgotha, the Place of a Skull (Matthew 27:33).

> As his twisted body hung on the cross it seemed to turn into a vast question mark against the sky line, and as from his mouth comes the cry, "My God, why?" it seems that all the anguish of the ages is gathered up in that bitter cry. There is not a single problem that perplexes and wrings our hearts that is not gathered up in that anguished question. How far can hate go? Why does the universe tolerate injustice? Why are the good seemingly deserted in their hour of anguish? Will the universe back good men?[44]

---

[44]E. Stanley Jones, *Christ and Human Suffering* (New York, NY: The Abington Press, 1933), 223.

Everywhere and relentlessly, Jesus was hounded by moral and spiritual depravity. But evil would not win the day, for Jesus would trap evil at its own game. At the cross, something strange and wonderful took place, something shocking, something that no one could have anticipated. Kreeft writes:

> That God should take alienation away from man by inserting alienation into the very heart of God; that he should conquer evil by allowing it its supreme, unthinkable triumph, deicide, the introduction of death into the life of God, the God of life, the Immortal One; that He should destroy the power of evil by allowing it to destroy him–this is "the foolishness of God [that] is wiser than men, and the weakness of God [that] is stronger than men" (1 Corinthians 1:25).[45]

Blocher adds these masterful words:

> Evil is conquered because God turns it back on itself. He makes the supreme crime, the murder of the only righteous person, the very operation that abolishes sin. The manoeuvre is unprecedented. No more complete victory could be imagined. God responds in the indirect way that is perfectly suited to the ambiguity of evil. Evil, like a judoist, takes advantage of the power of the good, which it perverts; the Lord, the supreme champion, replies by using the very grip of the opponent. . . . At the cross, evil is conquered by the ultimate degree of love in the fulfillment of justice.[46]

In the death of Jesus, evil is somehow absorbed, and through His resurrection the efficacy of the cross is verified and its power released. Though this does not provide a solution to every imaginable question that plaques our souls, it does show us that the incarnate Lord has conquered evil in principle, and that our worst enemy cannot stand up to the wisdom and love of God. Says Jones:

---

[45]Peter Kreeft, *Making Sense Out of Suffering* (Ann Arbor, MI: Servant Books, 1986), 132.

[46]Blocher, *Evil and the Cross*, 132-133.

Jesus let life speak its cruelest word, so that the gentlest and purest heart that ever beat was stilled in death, and then he quietly rose from the dead, came forth from the tomb with the most tremendous words ever uttered upon his lips: "I am the resurrection and the life." It is this that gives the whole thing point, for it sets the sorrows of life to music and makes the ultimate note to be joy.[47]

The implications of this divine mission are staggering. For one, Jesus is the supreme paradigm of right living. His willingness to endure evil for the sake of God's glory is both an incentive and a pattern. Like Him, every Christian must take up his cross (Mark 8:34). This is the life of God's people in this world.

Of course Jesus' life, death, and resurrection also provide hope, as He will one day physically re-enter this world (Mark 13:26-27). The redemptive accomplishments of Jesus ensure God's people that suffering will one day end (see chapter 9). Temporary struggles, as intense and painful as they can be, will eventually be replaced by unfathomable bliss (Revelation 21:1-4).

The cross teaches us other things as well, for through it God gives a grand demonstration of wisdom, His ability to solve what appears to human beings an insuperable problem. There are many implications to consider. Of primary concern is the matter of human rebellion and redemption. Both the Bible and honest self-reflection indicate human guilt, and there are no obvious ways in which a holy God can establish a relationship with those who have violated His will. At the same time, the Scriptures declare God's determination to rescue those who are lost and blameworthy. This places God in quite a predicament, for one wonders how God can demonstrate love toward the unrighteous without compromising His righteous standards.

But God is not stumped, having planned all along to send a substitute, One who would live and die on behalf of others (Isaiah 53; Mark 10:45). Here is a clear case, then, in which God provides an answer where one seemed unavailable. Evil looked like the victor in the battle against God's Chosen One. But evil did not ultimately triumph. While scheming men

---

[47]Jones, *Christ and Human Suffering*, 224-225.

were nailing Jesus to a tree, Jesus was in effect nailing evil to that same wooden beam. Frame aptly summarizes:

> But here is the lesson for us: If God could vindicate His justice and mercy in a situation where such vindication seemed impossible, if He could vindicate them in a way that went far beyond our expectations and understanding, can we not trust Him to vindicate himself again? If God is able to provide an answer to the exceptionally difficult Old Testament form of the problem of evil, does it not make sense that he can and will answer our remaining difficulties? Does it not make sense to trust and obey, even in the midst of suffering?[48]

Again, it must be acknowledged that this component of a Christian theodicy does not get to the bottom of every imaginable problem about suffering, nor does it necessarily provide easy relief for human pain. Therefore, only partial answers are available, coupled with practical comforts and a strong incentive of hope. As to the problem of evil,

> [a] ray of light pierces the gloom. It comes from the cross. The impenetrable mystery of evil meets the paradoxical mystery of the cross. The mystery of Golgotha is that of the darkness which turns to light, as the Psalmist said, for God and for us - for us by God (Ps. 139:11ff). We understand that we cannot understand, and even a little more. At the cross, we find the verification of God's mastery over evil, of his incorporating it within his plan, of his using evil men, and of his freedom from all suspicion in complicity in it.[49]

Kreeft appropriately captures this thought: "We are finally led not to the answer but to the Answerer."[50] Through Jesus the mystery of evil is swallowed by the greater enigma of the cross. Indeed, in light of Jesus' resurrection, everything takes on a different hue.

---

[48]Frame, *Apologetics to the Glory of God*, 184. The form of the problem of evil to which Frame refers is that of the seeming impossibility of reconciling God's justice with His mercy. Paul takes up this theme in the book of Romans where he declares that Christ's death does just that (Romans 3:26).

[49]Blocher, *Evil and the Cross*, 130.

[50]Peter Kreeft, *Making Sense Out of Suffering*, 129.

When Jesus emerged from the tomb, justice, spirituality, relationship, and beauty rose with him. Something has happened in and through Jesus as a result of which the world is a different place, a place where heaven and earth have joined forever. God's future has arrived in the present. Instead of mere echoes, we hear the voice itself: a voice which speaks of rescue from evil and death, and hence a new creation.[51]

In God's unique Son, we find a foretaste of heaven, the anticipation of something wonderful, and the promise of evil's destruction. In Jesus there is safety now and the assurance that evil will one day be expelled from the lives of God's children. Then, evil will no longer be a problem.

---

[51]N. T. Wright, *Simply Christian: Why Christianity Makes Sense* (SanFrancisco, CA: HarperCollins Books, 2006), 116.

*"In the world you have tribulation, but take courage;
I have overcome the world."*

Jesus Christ

❦

Chapter 9

Coping with Evil

It is one thing to debate the abstract and theoretical but quite another to provide comfort and hope. "Theological concepts don't amount to very much unless they can speak to someone . . . who gropes for God's love in a world bordered by grief."[52] What we all need, then, is something that will enable us to cope with the tragedies that come our way. To that end the following remarks may prove useful.

1. Evil will not last forever.

The book of Revelation speaks of a day when God "will wipe away every tear from their eyes; and there will no longer be any death; there will no longer be any mourning, or crying, or pain; the first things have passed away" (Revelation 21:4). The "first things" mentioned here include heartache, tragedy, and a whole range of soul-crushing influences. These are the events that both hurt and baffle, causing millions to weep.

---

[52]Philip Yancey, *Disappointment with God: Three Questions No One Asks Aloud* (Grand Rapids, MI: Zondervan Publishing House, 1988), 180.

But better things await. While the author does not provide details as to when all of these eschatological events will transpire, he does clearly indicate that suffering is temporary and that evil will one day be removed.

Whether or not we are satisfied with any particular theodicy, what most of us crave is really quite simple; we desire life as it was intended to be, life that is purposeful and fulfilling. In the ultimate sense, this will take place when death and evil are abolished. Therefore, one of the best ways to endure trouble is by considering its temporariness. Though we struggle now, evil will not last forever. And when suffering finally comes to an end, only joy will remain. Our hope is anchored to that day (Revelation 21:20).

2. Future good easily outshines (and outlasts) present suffering.

Imagine for a moment the terrible scars resulting from the presence of evil. Contemplate the misery endured by millions. Consider the innumerable injustices that have occurred throughout time. Evil has left an indelible mark. Yet, here is a remarkable thing. According to Paul, "The sufferings of this present time are not worthy to be compared with the glory that is to be revealed to us" (Romans 8:18). "Not worthy to be compared" coveys the idea of one thing so surpassing another that the lesser of the two is not even in the same category. But, amazingly, the "lesser thing" spoken of here is suffering.

It is clear that Paul in no way minimizes evil. Quite the contrary, he intends to show how incredible the future will be by contrasting it with our most formidable enemy, the worst of human (and divine!) foes. On the one side, there is this scoundrel called suffering. On the other is unimaginable glory. What we are told is that future bliss is of such magnitude that evil–even evil!–is shown to be trivial, small, insignificant, "not worthy to be compared."

If future good so outshines present evil, believers are given strong motivation to persevere and to bask in the implications of this promise. Evil is no small thing, but it fades in the presence of God. Job found this to be the case. Though he never received an answer to his troubles, God's presence satisfied him. This is why Job's response was one of repentance and wonder. "God does not overwhelm Job with an irrefutable case for divine goodness and wisdom. God overwhelms Job with majesty, yes, as an argument to warrant Job's deferential trust."[53]

How great the Lord must be to so easily outmatch evil, and how encouraged we should be with the thought. Evil is immense but not when compared with the glory that is to be revealed. Indeed, how incredible it is to consider that believers will participate in this resplendent experience of utter satisfaction.

3. It is possible and reasonable to find comfort, even when many answers are not available.

As mentioned above, Job did not receive a direct explanation for his troubles. But perhaps that was not what he required. Often it is the case that the deepest need of the hurting is not intellectual precision but emotional consolation. It is proper, therefore, for Christians, even questioning, doubting Christians, to take advantage of the comforting provisions God has made.

Many grieving individuals have been sustained through close friendships (fellowship), a close dependence on God (prayer), and a willingness to reflect (meditation) on the promises of God. Intellectual matters are certainly not to be despised, as they can provide further impetus for continuance in the faith. But in the final analysis, the Spirit is able to sustain us even when we lack satisfactory answers. In fact divine transcendence (God's "aboveness") is itself a driving force in spiritual growth, for it forces us to depend on the One who alone is "the way, and the truth, and the life" (John 14:6). This, I would submit, is ultimately a good thing.

4. In the rescuing work of Jesus, God has already demonstrated His immeasurable love and the ability to solve inscrutable problems.

Jesus is described in Scripture as the Alpha and Omega (Revelation 22:13), which includes the notion that He is "Lord of all that happens in human

---

[53]Stackhouse, *Can God Be Trusted?* 98.

history."[54] From beginning to end, He is the centerpiece of genuine spirituality. As our sympathetic high priest, He has been tested like all people (Hebrews 4:14-16). And through His life, death, and resurrection, the love of God has been manifested to the fullest degree. As a result, He supplies His followers with salvific assurance, spiritual stability, legitimate hope, intense and uninterrupted friendship, and a tenderness of which the world is unaware.

It is with good cause, then, that we learn to look to and depend on Him. If God has given the greatest of gifts, His Son, surely He will not forget the beneficiaries of His grace (Romans 8:32). As we encounter the mysteries of life, our hope is located in the God who is able to buttress us with His presence, a keen awareness of His love, and confidence enough that He will see us through to the end (Philippians 1:6).

5. Due to our own frailty and imperfection, we need God if we are to make any real sense of the world in which we live.

One of the ironies inherent in the problem of evil is the fact that, apart from God, there is no way in which evil can be understood, much less opposed. Only if there is a supreme standard-Giver can we even begin to use the language of "right and wrong." Thus, even though evil is thought to be an argument against the existence of a sovereign and good supreme being, the fact that we even find evil objectionable hints at the reality of God. Quite bluntly, if there is no God, then evil becomes impossible to identify. Indeed, how can we even complain about evil if we live in a Godless world?

None of this means, of course, that evil is easily explained, for it is not. However, it does go a long way to showing that the very recognition of something called evil is actually an argument in favor of an evil-opposing deity. Now, if this is the case, then it makes sense that in our efforts to construct a theodicy, we should actively seek His presence.

---

[54]George Eldon Ladd, *A Commentary on the Revelation of John* (Grand Rapids, MI: William B. Eerdmans Publishing Company, 1972), 29. Alpha and Omega, the first and last letters of the Greek alphabet, signify that God is before all things and will outlast everything. As such, it is an appropriate description of deity. Hebrews says something similar when it describes Jesus as "the author and perfecter of faith" (Hebrews 12:2).

Thus, while in one sense we object to what God's providence allows, in another sense, we need His assistance if ever we are going to move in a helpful direction. As Newbigin remarks:

> We are *not* honest and open-minded explorers who formulate the real questions in a search for a yet-to-be-discovered reality; we are alienated from reality because we have made ourselves the center of the universe. Before we continue with our questions, we have to answer a question put to us from the heart of the mystery. We have to answer that anguished question, "Adam, where are you?" We have to learn that we are lost and that we have to be rescued. We have to answer the call of the one who has come to rescue us and learn that it is only in him and through him that we shall be led into the truth in its fullness.[55]

Somehow, this tension, a fierce commitment to faith coupled with a willingness to express hurt and doubt, must be sustained. Though we writhe in pain as we state our objections, it is not likely that we will make much headway unless we rely upon the One to whom we complain. This strange and ironic situation does not supply an end to our difficulties but it does provide "the way" (John 14:6).

---

[55]Leslie Newbigin, *Proper Confidence: Faith, Doubt, and Certainty in Christian Discipleship* (Grand Rapids, MI: William B. Eerdmans Publishing Company, 1995), 104.

"Not only is another world possible, she is on her way. On a quiet day, I can hear her breathing."

Arundhati Roy

Chapter 10

Evil in a Postmodern Era

Society is experiencing a monumental cultural shift as it moves from a modern to a postmodern paradigm. While some within the church have taken postmodern themes to an extreme, it is perhaps more common for believers to remain distant from recent trends, or to oppose cultural tendencies that are seen as a threat to truth and spirituality.

While it is essential to resist error, it is also important to consider those features of postmodern thought that might assist those struggling with the presence of evil in a good God's world. Though it is beyond the scope of this work to offer a detailed critique of postmodernism,[56] there are some broad ideas that warrant our inspection. Before proceeding, however, it is

---

[56]For further information on postmodernism and related subjects, see Stanley J. Grenz, *A Primer on Postmodernism* (Grand Rapids, MI: William B. Eerdmans Publishing Company, 1996), Leonard Sweet, *Postmodern Pilgrims: First Century Passion For the 21ˢᵗ Century World* (Nashville, TN: Broadman & Holman Press, 2000), Chuck Smith, Jr., *The End of the World As We Know It: Clear Direction for Bold and Innovative Ministry in a Postmodern World* (Colorado Springs, CO: WaterBrook Press, 2001), *Christianity and the Postmodern Turn: Six Views*, ed. Myron B. Penner (Grand Rapids, MI: Brazos Press, 2005), and Carmen C. DiCello, *Dangerous Blessing: The Emergence of a Postmodern Faith* (Eugene, OR: Wipf & Stock Publishers, 2005).

crucial to recognize that, contrary to the opinions of certain philosophers, there is indeed such a thing as evil in the first place.

Evil Persists

Certain postmoderns have followed a line of thought which leads to the rejection of universally applicable standards. Thus, the truth claims of previous generations are reinterpreted as mere points of view. What was once deemed right or wrong is now considered the opinion of an individual or a local community.

Though some have gone to this extreme, promoting a type of deconstruction that leads to relativism, life has a way of coaxing us back to reality. For instance even the most determined relativist tends to compromise his philosophy when confronted with evil. When an atheist is unfairly treated or an agnostic is physically attacked, the philosophy of "no moral absolutes" loses much of its punch.

It would seem, in other words, that God has built the world in such a way that we all hear at least an echo of His voice. While it may be more difficult to discern precise parameters of morality than some moderns have been willing to admit, it is also true that we act, instinctively and almost universally, as if there are some standards. One needs only think of slavery in America or the atrocities of Autzwitz to realize that, official disclaimers to the contrary, some things are just plain wrong. It is at this level, therefore, that no rhetoric of getting beyond good and evil can satisfy the human soul.

Thus, even the most radical of postmoderns must acknowledge evil, especially when it gets personal. While generally careful not to provide a detailed moral code, postmoderns are compelled to live within (if not also acknowledge) a framework for ethical behavior.

If this is the case, if there is still within the heart of postmodern society an acknowledgment of evil, what postmodern themes can aid us in developing a theodicy? More so, how might wounded hearts experience a measure of solace? What follows are some suggestions that are both postmodern in orientation and, more importantly, biblical in focus.[57]

---

[57]One of the more important things that cultural trends can do is drive us back to our sacred texts. If God is active in the world (and He is), we should look for Him,

Postmodern Themes and a Christian Theodicy

Postmodern motifs include an increased emphasis on community, an alertness to the limitations inherent in all human knowing, a genuine desire to experience truth (and not merely hypothesize about it), a captivation with stories (as opposed to propositions alone), and a tendency to treat life more like a journey toward the truth than an arrival at the truth. Each of these deserves further attention.

Community and the Sharing of Grief

Many today are captivated by community and driven by the friendships it provides. Though human beings have always needed to connect with others, postmoderns are particularly concerned to find places of belonging. As a result, there is much emphasis on this theme.

This community orientation is something that is embedded in Scripture, finding its impetus in the fact that human beings are created in the image of a communing God.

> The fact that God is the social trinity—Father, Son, and Spirit—gives us some indication that the divine purpose for creation is directed toward the individual-in-relationship. Our gospel must address the human person within the context of the communities in which people are embedded.[58]

Just as, according to Christian theology, God is a plurality of persons, a divine community of interaction, so we are wired to commune. It is thus no surprise to find that most people desire to lives their lives in conjunction with those who are likeminded.

As for the problem of evil, Scripture is replete with examples of how this is to take place. When the early church was scattered due to persecution, there was a strong impetus to provide a haven for those who had lost everything. As

---

contemplating what we observe from within a Scriptural frame of reference. To the degree that God is operating in this postmodern phase of history, we must investigate current themes in light of His Word.

[58]Stanley J. Grenz, *A Primer on Postmodernism* (Grand Rapids, MI: William B. Eerdmans Publishing Company, 1996), 168-169.

Acts describes, "all those who had believed were together and had all things in common" (Acts 2:44). This is summarized by Paul, who instructs his readers to "Be devoted to one another in brotherly love" (Romans 12:10), which includes a willingness to "weep with those who weep" (Romans 12:15).

What this means, practically, is that we all need a place where we can mourn, a sanctuary in which we can give expression to our hurt, pain, and doubt. Though the church has sometimes hindered this process by creating unrealistic expectations for its people, Scripture teaches and postmodernism confirms that it is reasonable and necessary to give voice to our complaints. Though all hurting individuals need time to be alone (some more than others), an ideal setting for grief and for grappling with the problem of evil is a body of empathetic believers (co-complainers?), a community in which believers are granted permission to take their pain and confusion into the presence of a compassionate God. Rather than denying us this right, as some overly dogmatic and unnecessarily strict Christians often do, the Church must learn to facilitate such soul-mending encounters.[59]

A Mystery within a Mystery

Moderns had (have) a tendency to approach life in a rather dogmatic fashion, treating some of the more difficult questions of truth and life as if they were easily answerable. Part of this is understandable, for God has indeed revealed Himself to His people. Given that He is a God of truth, it makes sense that we would be confident about what He has shared with us.

That God is a revealing God is no surprise to Christians. On the other hand, believers have not always been cognizant of the concomitant reality that many things about God are not so easily deciphered. Though He has revealed many truths to us, "the secret things" are hidden from our view. The Lord is a deity who both reveals *and* conceals (see Deuteronomy 29:29).

Postmoderns, some of whom have grown skeptical of overly confident claims, tend to reject anything that sounds too dogmatic, (sometimes to the point of embracing outright skepticism), preferring a humbler approach

---

[59]For a fascinating look at the various dimensions of community, see Joseph R. Myers, *The Search to Belong: Rethinking Intimacy, Community, and Small Groups* (Grand Rapids, MI: Zondervan Publishing Company, 2003).

to knowledge. This does not mean that postmoderns themselves are necessarily more humble than their predecessors. It does mean, however, that their general philosophy of life is one in which close mindedness and unnecessarily narrow views are despised.

This dovetails nicely into a Christian worldview. Scripture not only provides parameters for living and truths for believing, but it also declares that many things defy the creature. One avenue by which we can approach the problem of evil, therefore, entails a recognition, even an embrace, of this fact of human ignorance in the presence of God. A Christian theodicy is fortified by the notion that we can only grasp deity in part, and that the Lord of Scripture will always exceed any efforts to comprehensively understand Him.

The mystery of the problem of evil, then, can be placed within the broader concept of the mystery of God Himself (see Chapter 7). Would it not be more conducive to building relationships with others for us to admit that there are often times when we, too, "don't get it"? Indeed, when we come to understand that it is valid to express our frustration ("Why does God do some of the things He does?") and admit our ignorance ("There are many things about God that I do not comprehend!"), we open ourselves up to (and model for others) a biblical perspective in which authenticity and genuine spirituality coexist. It is possible, in other words, to be honest (even disappointed) and yet still experience a satisfying and faithful relationship with God. When we cannot fathom, we can at least rest in the One whose goodness and magnificence demand a reverent response. Isaiah puts it this way: "But to this one I will look, to him who is humble and contrite of spirit, and who trembles at My word" (66:2).

Experiencing the Truth

During the modern era, the temptation was to spend an inordinate amount of time and energy constructing theories, sometimes mistaking meaning for application and confusing knowledge about God with an actual acquaintance with Him. Clearly, both of these are needed if we are going to live in accordance with the Bible. That is, there is a relationship between the ideas we hold *about* God and the relationship we establish *with* Him. Still, with the church's determination to remain doctrinally sound and theologically informed, the personal matter of connecting with God was sometimes minimized.[60]

81

In contrast, postmoderns have a deep sense of wanting to encounter the truth and not merely formulate theories about it. There is, as might be expected, a tendency to go too far in the other direction and to neglect theory in favor of practice. Still, the postmodern desire to experience the transcendent is indeed a healthy impulse.

The Bible in many places assumes this personal encounter with the truth. Paul, for instance, makes clear his passion for God as "knowing Him" (Philippians 3:10). Likewise, Peter speaks of growing "in the grace and knowledge of our Lord and Savior" (2 Peter 3:18), and John writes of possessing life *through the Son* (1 John 5:11-12 - "having the Son" is the way he puts it). In all of these passages, *descriptive knowledge of God* intersects with a *personal encounter with God.* Our efforts, therefore, must be directed toward not only providing accurate information but actually looking to the One who is "not far from each one of us" (Acts 17:27).

Concerning a Christian theodicy, this theme reminds us that, while intellectual matters are certainly relevant, the key to surviving difficulty and being able to live amid evil is related to our union with our Maker. While we can and should seek answers to questions about suffering, what all people require, as Scripture affirms, is an ongoing encounter with God.

Participating in the Story

One key feature of postmodern thought is its fascination with narrative. While moderns were drawn to propositions, postmoderns are attracted to stories. From the vantage point of the Bible, this is very significant, for a good portion of Scripture takes this form. From the story of the nation of Israel to the accounts of the early church, the narrative sections of Scripture play a vital role. Indeed, Jesus' ministry was often driven by this story-telling agenda, sharing parables with the people of His day (Matthew 22:1ff; Mark 4:1ff).

It is with good reason, therefore, that the church learns to reemphasize this narrative approach. Rather than treating the stories of Scripture as pointers to abstract propositions, as mere addendums to biblical doctrines, the stories themselves become essential features of the church's mission.

---

[60]One obvious exception to this trend is found among Pentecostal and Charismatic believers, who have always emphasized the relational.

Of course the postmodern penchant for story does not, in itself, guarantee any type of spiritual benefit. It does, however, provide ample reason for believing that human beings are "wired" for story.

> The business of the church is to tell and to embody a story, the story of God's mighty acts in creation and redemption and of God's promises concerning what will be in the end. The church affirms the truth of this story by celebrating it, interpreting it, and enacting it in the life of the contemporary world.[61]

Concerning a theodicy, there are hints in Scripture that might assist us along the way. One of these would be a recounting of those stories in which God's people encountered, survived, and even thrived during times of unspeakable evil. For instance, as one contemplates the story of Joseph's mistreatment, it is easy to recognize both the degree of suffering he endured and the amazing way he handled hard circumstances (Genesis 50:20). Likewise, the New Testament provides many instances detailing the church's persecution and hardship (Acts 8:1; 2 Thessalonians 1:4; 2 Timothy 3:12). And the greatest example of faithful persistence amid evil is that of Jesus (Matthew 26:36-46); as the biblical writers take up this theme, our duty is to allow these passages to impact our thoughts and lives.

In each of these examples, a story is told in which God's people successfully, albeit painfully, cope with evil. Though no single answer is given for the unfair circumstances of life, this narrative environment provides inspired accounts of others who encountered suffering. Somehow, as our stories intersect those of the biblical characters, we find comfort. Though we still have questions, we are at least provided an atmosphere in which the same God who acted in the past can intervene in our lives today.

Journeying Toward Comfort

Some within the church place an emphasis on what might be termed immediate transformation. A crisis experience or a decision is held out as the pathway to imminent blessing. If we have needs, a "power encounter"

---

[61]Leslie Newbigin, *Proper Confidence*, 76.

can occur in which the Holy Spirit alters hearts, changes perspectives, and enables people to see their own lives from a different perspective.

No one who wants to be faithful to Scripture can deny the possibility of such encounters. Certainly, God has and can intervene in our lives in such a way as to radically change us. This "here and how" approach is not to be despised, for none of us can predict how God will work to encourage His children. There is little doubt, therefore, that the living Lord can and does provide direct and sometimes spontaneous aid.

On the other hand, some traditional Christians have taken this instant transformation model too far, treating spirituality as primarily a series of encounters and neglecting to see that it is also a journey. Postmoderns resonate with this gradual approach, recognizing that life, including one's spiritual life, usually entails a process. Paul sounds this theme when he describes the life of faith as something to be "worked out" over time (Philippians 2:12ff). Likewise, Peter speaks of ongoing diligence and growth as the pattern for Jesus' disciples (2 Peter 3:14-18).

When encountering evil, therefore, it is important to not only look to God expectantly for immediate assistance (which we have already mentioned above, and which God does provide) but to realize, as well, that both our experience of consolation and our recognition of what God is "up to" are matters to be worked out over a lifetime. However exaggerated it may be, it is in one sense true that "time heals." Or, from a biblical-theological perspective, it is better to say that *God* heals over time.

Conclusion

The subjects addressed here are a mere sampling of themes that contribute to a postmodern perspective on theodicy. As God is sovereign in every era, and due to the fact that He has seen fit to direct us in this postmodern way, it is incumbent upon the church to listen for His voice as it reverberates across time. With a healthy openness to what God is doing in our world today, combined with a commitment to the "once for all" nature of the Christian faith, it is possible to benefit from current societal inclinations. In the process, we receive the comfort and the guidance we all so desperately need.

"When we cannot trace God's hand,
we simply must trust His heart."

C. H. Spurgeon

Chapter 11

Conclusion

Those who seriously consider the depth and intensity of evil in this world are not likely to treat it lightly. This is especially true among men and women who have experienced it first hand. The desperate agony, the nagging questions, the ongoing confusion–these are what make evil a problem in the first place.

It is astonishing, then, to find some treating this subject in flippant ways, minimizing the ugliness and profound horror of it all, spouting off simplistic answers that hardly meet the needs of the human heart. Of course a part of this is due to the fact that no one likes to ponder too long over that which is painful. This is why some ignore the topic altogether, while others try to overly simplify. Kelly James Clark puts it this way:

> "Beginning to think," Camus writes, "is beginning to be undermined." It is difficult to imagine a better word. All of our self-constructed securities crumble and give way beneath us. We precipitously fall–into what? The old pat answers give no comfort; they no longer seem to work. Our lives are propped up with feeble justifications, rationalizations, and clichés that give way under the weight of human experience.[62]

---

[62]Kelly James Clark, *When Faith is Not Enough* (Grand Rapids, MI: William B. Eerdmans Publishing Company, 1997), 113.

When it comes to evil, the Bible is remarkably up-to-date and forthright. The biblical writers never shy away from the troubles of life, often portraying suffering as a puzzling thing. From the anguish of Job to the distress of the Thessalonian believers, life in the real world can be devastating. Intellectual difficulties seem not to go away, and heartache appears an unshakable foe. With countless believers down through the ages, the question still emerges: "Why?"

But the honesty and frustration so common in the Bible must not be construed in such a way that skepticism and hopelessness thrive. Quite the contrary, the authors of Scripture are dedicated to showing that hope can survive in a fallen world.

Among a number of factors, a Christian theodicy is theocentric, allowing the immensity of evil to be viewed from the perspective of the greater transcendent-immanent God. Though pain is enormous, we accept by faith that God is bigger still. This does not lead to a full explanation of evil, but it does provide a measure of the stability, motivation, and hope necessary for navigating hard times.

Another major theme in Scripture concerns the end of time, when current difficulties will (for God's people) be replaced by ineffable joy. Evil is confusing now, but it will one day be destroyed. Over and again, we are enjoined to look forward with anticipation to that day. Whether or not every question is answered, it is comforting to know that Jesus' followers "will be like Him, because [they] will see Him just as He is" (1 John 3:2-3). In the meantime hope can indeed have a purifying affect.

Of course most significant to the Bible's point of view is the cross of God's Son; in Him evil is overcome. Does this take away all of the pain? Obviously not. But enough answers are given, as the love and power of Jesus' death become a great balm for those damaged by suffering. Evil is smothered by the awe-inspiring spectacle of God on a cross. As Bloesch states: "We do not have the truth in its ultimacy, but we know the One who is the truth, and our task is to point others to this One who alone can resolve their difficulties and bind their wounds."[63]

Disciples of Jesus are provided ample support for enduring the heart wrenching obstacles of life. Those who trust and obey, and who think

---

[63]Donald G. Bloesch, *A Theology of Word & Spirit: Authority and Method in Theology* (Downers Grove, IL: InterVarsity Press, 1992), 23.

and pray through the implications of a biblical worldview, receive support from the hand of the gracious Lord who promises to wipe every tear away (Revelation 21:3-4).

In light of the many puzzling features of human existence in a fallen world, true consolation can only come from the revealing-concealing God, who invites us to follow His counsel where we can and to rest in His presence (even when He seems absent). Even when we are surrounded by darkness, a light appears in the distance and the figure of the cross comes into view. It is in Him that the mystery of evil is finally vanquished from our lives by the power of incarnate love.

"One deep and serious groan is more acceptable to God than the creation of a world."

Thomas Traherne

Appendix A

1 Peter 3:15 and an Apologetic of Hope

Sanctify Christ as Lord in your hearts, always being ready to make a defense to everyone who asks you to give an account for the hope that is in you, yet with gentleness and reverence.

The goal of apologetics is no more clearly stated than in 1 Peter 3:15. Here, the task of offering a reason for our hope is delineated. This "defense" of Christianity includes a proper commitment to Jesus, as well as a concerted effort to provide a rationale for faith.

Of special significance to this discussion is the context from which this letter is written. Peter's audience includes those who have experienced rejection for Jesus' sake, having been "distressed by various trials" (1:6). This suffering, we are told, mirrors that of Jesus (2:21-25).

Living within such a hostile environment, it is understandable that Christians would need a measure of encouragement. Peter meets this need by anchoring their hope to their Savior. To suffer for Him is an honor and blessing (3:14).

It is interesting to consider the manner in which Peter instructs these suffering believers. Not only does he help to stabilize them in the faith, but he instructs them, amid hard times, to display an attitude in which the gospel is advanced and the truth defended. Even as dark situations present themselves, Jesus' followers are to be "giv[ing] an account for the hope that is in [them]" (3:15).

The fact is, God's people were never promised a painless existence. Had this been the case, Peter would not have depicted his readers in such woeful condition (3:14). They were clearly hurting individuals. But–and this is the point–they were also much more, for they retained a strong hope. Hope, in other words, had fortified their lives. As a result, outsiders took notice.

What Peter is saying, therefore, is that we can use our very worst life-situations as platforms for reaching those currently outside of the faith. Though Christians grieve like everyone else, their grief is unlike the world's. When this hope is expressed, those outside of the faith take notice, perhaps wondering what makes these believers so different. Thus, a type of evangelistic opportunity is provided. Whatever level of pain and bewilderment a Christian faces, others are watching. Through the tears, Peter tells us, it is possible to exude hope and show others of what this hope consists.

It is in this sense that even the frustrations and struggles of life, though still baffling, are one of God's current ways of showing forth the light of His love and the hope of a better tomorrow. Here, then, is an apologetic strategy that depends not initially on reasoned argumentation but on the God-given ability to see, even amid darkness, that Jesus is the true light of the world (John 1:9; 9:5; 11:9). As Jesus Himself put it: "I have come as Light into the world, so that everyone who believes in Me will not remain in darkness" (12:46).

Appendix B

Additional Musings on the
Proper Response to Mystery

God has built mystery into the fiber of the universe. On the one hand, the divine handiwork is evident for all who care to see (Psalm 19:1-6; Romans 1:19-20). On the other hand, even what we know is shrouded in mystery. Take, for example, the biblical doctrine of the Trinity. The Bible clearly teaches that God is both three and one (Isaiah 48:16 and Deuteronomy 6:4). Yet, no one truly comprehends all that this means. Then, there is Jesus; He is both divine and human (Colossians 2:9). But, once again, this truth is unfathomable. Plainly, God's intention includes both disclosure and hiddenness.

It is at this point that some are tripped up and led to believe that partial knowledge (and so partial ignorance) somehow detracts from a biblical worldview. But this is not necessary the case. Indeed, there are lessons to be learned not only from what is seen but from what is not. Among these are a deepened faith and a heightened sense of appreciation for who and what God is.

Biblical faith has substance in that it rests on the reliable Word of God, which is coherent and consistent. At the same time, faith involves mystery, for the God of Scripture can sometimes *appear* as if He is not being consistent. It is not that He is whimsical or untrustworthy, for He is the epitome of reliability. There are times, though, when He *seems* to contradict Himself. When this occurs, it is important to recall what we know about God, both from Scripture and personal experience, and then entrust ourselves to Him despite our circumstances.

A number of suggestions have already been given as to why He chooses to act in this way. Part of our difficulty, no doubt, is due to the fact that God's ways far exceed our own (Isaiah 46:5). It would be unrealistic to expect a created being to grasp everything about the uncreated and eternal One. There are times when God goes out of His way to highlight this fact for us.

Here, then, is what we are left to deal with: (1) God is good and fair. (2) But sometimes He doesn't seem to be good and fair. As a result, we are left to "scratch our heads," wondering how to reconcile what we know about God with God's own providence. (3) The trick, or so it seems, is to accept (by faith) that His ways do indeed make sense, even when we can't discern how. This way, we allow our ignorance to incite worship, not doubt. More so, even our doubts can facilitate our sense of adoration. At the end of the day, we remain dumbfounded before a God who is perfectly good and just, even though it is impossible to tie together every loose end.

As we come to grips with our own ignorance, we are forced to trust the Lord. Not only is He reliable when life makes sense. He can (and must) be trusted when nothing makes sense. Our inability to master deity is an indication of His transcendent greatness and an incentive to worship. In the end, therefore, mystery needn't lead people away from God in horror and doubt. Instead, it can reinforce what we already know about our good and faithful Lord.

Appendix C

Is Evil Really a Mystery?

One of the basic premises of this study is that evil is at some level a mystery. This does not mean that one is left clueless when it come to understanding these matters. Neither does mystery imply illogic or a pessimistic outlook. In fact mystery has an important role to play in the way we perceive God (see chapter 7).

But there are certain Christians who are not so quick to relegate suffering to this category. To be frank, some have spent too much time and energy convincing others of their "airtight arguments" to have to admit that there really is a whole lot of mystery when it comes to the faith. Thus, this idea is either ignored or downplayed. After all, we "knowers" simply cannot allow very much emphasis on what we do not know.[64]

Contrary to these overly confident apologists, this researcher believes it is possible to have partial answers to the problem of evil, while recognizing,

---

[64]Some segments of the church portray the faith in an almost Gnostic fashion, treating their particular belief systems as nearly flawless, and acting like they have inside information not available to others. Like the early Gnostics (from the Greek *gnosis*, meaning "to know"), these Christians are so confident in their ability to discern hidden insights that they begin to treat their interpretations in a dogmatic fashion. Though the truth is sufficiently perspicuous and discoverable, it is essential to pursue it with an attitude of deep humility.

as well, that much mystery remains. As explained earlier, admitting to such mystery is not at all a bad thing. To make this point, it might help to get the perspective of those who have made contributions to a Christian theodicy. What follows are the opinions of a number of thinkers on this subject.

David Atkinson says:

> there are more things in heaven and earth than we have ever dreamt of.
> . . . There are uncertainties, puzzles and ambiguities in the life of faith which we have to leave with the mystery of God. "The secret things belong to the Lord." We must allow God to have his secrets, and receive from him the gift of faith to hold into him in our uncertainties. . . . May God deepen our faith, even when we are in the dark.[65]

Henri Blocher states bluntly:

> Scripture teaches us that we shall not find, at least in this life, the rationale solution that so many have sought after. It does not give us the answer. In fact it goes much further than that: it turns its floodlights onto the difficulty, and invites us to take a different step. This is at least one of the purposes of the book of Job.[66]

Blocher adds:

> The sovereignty of God, which is affirmed times without number in his own revelation, makes his permission of evil an impenetrable mystery.[67]

Tucker provides these words of wisdom:

> Recognizing and appreciating God as mystery–as opposed to God as defined by facts and proofs–can be an important step in coming to terms

---

[65]David Atkinson, *The Message of Job* (Downers Grove, IL: InterVarsity Press, 1991), 160.
[66]Blocher, *Evil and the Cross*, 101.
[67]Ibid., 129.

with doubt and unbelief. God's hiddenness and absence make sense only in the context of mystery.[68]

Donald G. Bloesch, writing about the limitations of human reason, writes:

[P]aradox keeps our theology humble, forcing us to acknowledge that the reality about which we speak cannot be mastered by human reasoning.[69]

John G. Stackhouse, Jr., commenting specifically on the subject of evil, says:

Sometime evil seems only a dark, disgusting mystery. We ought to confront the possibility that there is not, and will not ever be, a humanly satisfactory explanation for this or that particular instance of evil, nor for the whole complex of evil in the world.[70]

D. A. Carson concurs, noting the example of Job:

Job teaches us that, at least in this world, there will always remain some mysteries to suffering.[71]

Summarizing a biblical view, Carson says:

we conclude that God tells us a great deal about evil and suffering. But the mysteries that remain are not going be answered at a merely theoretical and intellectual level.[72]

---

[68]Ruth A. Tucker, *Walking Away from Faith: Unraveling the Mystery of Belief and Unbelief* (Downers Grove, IL: InterVarsity Press, 2002), 65.
[69]Bloesch, *A Theology of Word & Spirit*, 79.
[70]Stackhouse, *Can God Be Trusted?* 63.
[71]Carson, *How Long, O Lord?* 174.
[72]Ibid., 245.

Kelly James Clark comments on Job:

> The free-will theodicy, which is so popular among philosophers and theologians, fails to explain all the wickedness and human suffering that there is in the world. God is telling Job that much more is at stake–but what? This we are not told. We awake again to mystery.[73]

Craig A. Loscalzo reflects the perspective of apologetics:

> So from the beginning we must admit that when we talk about matters of God and faith, some things are beyond our finite comprehension and understanding. That does not mean that we believe out of ignorance or live in darkness. Our understanding is based on faith. And our faith is suffused with wonder and mystery.[74]

In the context of Asaph's words in Psalm 13. Ferguson writes:

> Asaph gives us a limited theodicy. He recognizes that life is filled with mystery. While he believes that God understands all things, Asaph knows he does not.[75]

John Frame, agreeing with VanTil, expresses it this way:

> Essentially, Van Til's theology is an appeal to God's inscrutable wisdom. God has the answer, but he has not chosen to reveal it to us, at least not comprehensively. Our thinking must be subject to his revelation, and where that revelation is silent, we must be silent as well.[76]

---

[73]Clark, *When Faith is Not Enough*, 86.
[74]Craig A. Loscalzo, *Apologetic Preaching: Proclaiming Christ to a Postmodern World* (Downers Grove, IL: InterVarsity Press, 200), 33.
[75]Sinclair B. Ferguson, *Deserted by God?* (Grand Rapids, MI: Baker Books, 1995), 85.
[76]John M. Frame, *Cornelius Van Til: An Analysis of His Thought* (Phillipsburg, NJ: Presbyterian and Reformed Publishing Company, 1995), 85.

J. I. Packer offers these words of advice:

> The safest way in theodicy is to leave God's permission of sin and moral evil as a mystery, and to reason from the good achieved in redemption.[77]

James Emery White says:

> While I struggle with the mystery that surrounds God, deep down I want God to be more than I am, to know more than I do. I yearn for God to be beyond my understanding.[78]

Philip Yancey writes:

> From the biblical evidence, I must conclude that any hard-and-fast answers to the "Why?" questions are, simply, out of reach.[79]

Brian D. McLaren strikes a nice balance, saying:

> A naive mind thinks that life is a problem to be solved through easy answers. The disillusioned mind, tired of easy answers, thinks life is a paradox to be accepted with willpower (or, negatively, with resignation). The seeking mind thinks that behind the superficial problems and apparent paradoxes, life is at heart a mystery to be explored, using faith.[80]

---

[77]J. I. Packer, "Theodicy" in *New Dictionary of Theology*, eds. Sinclair B. Ferguson, David F. Wright (Downers Grove, IL: InterVarsity Press, 1988), 679.
[78]James Emery White, *Embracing the Mysterious God: Loving the God We Don't Understand* (Downers Grove, IL: InterVarsity Press, 2003), 105.
[79]Philip Yancey, *Disappointment With God*, 226.
[80]Brian D. McLaren, *The Church on the Other Side: Doing Ministry in the Postmodern Matrix* (Grand Rapids, MI: Zondervan Publishing House, 2000), 79.

Of course the rightness or wrongness of one's view cannot be determined by merely gathering together the opinions of men. It is perhaps helpful, though, to realize that others share a similar outlook. With these thoughts in mind, it is hoped that the reader will search these and similar resources to decide whether the arguments presented here are reflective of a biblical worldview.

Appendix D

Thoughts on Personal Evil

One of the dangers in looking at the problem of evil is the tendency to turn one's attention merely outward. While there is much evil "out there," and though evil is baffling, it is important to remember the personal side of this enigma. In the words of Pogo, the satirical cartoon figure from the fifties: "We have met the enemy, and he is us."

Everywhere the Bible affirms this reality of human rebellion and moral twistedness. Humanity is variously labeled as "under sin" (Romans 3:9), "hostile toward God" (Romans 8:7), "under a curse" (Galatians 3:10), "dead in trespasses and sins" (Ephesians 2:1), and "in the power of the evil one" (1 John 5:19). While these depictions are of the unconverted, and though the Christian is "a new creature" (2 Corinthians 5:17), the general tendency to rebel and act unwisely remains in all of us. Even those who claim to be the Lord's are quite capable of being "caught in [a] trespass" (Galatians 6:1), causing disharmony (Philippians 4:2), and misinterpreting God's ways (Galatians 2:11).

Whatever other considerations come to mind, the problem of evil is man's moral problem. However, troubling evil may appear, more troubling still is the human heart, which is "more deceitful than all else" (Jeremiah 17:9). Due to these factors, a number of significant truths should occupy the thoughts of anyone seeking to provide a Christian theodicy. Among these are the following:

1. Humanity's perception of life, including the evil that abounds, is at some level misguided or skewed due to the human propensity to mistake what God has done or said. See chapter 2.

2. Apart from spiritual renovation and divine wisdom, there is little hope of achieving an optimal theodicy (John 3:3ff; 1 Corinthians 2:1ff). Quite frankly, we need God and His Word to even begin to make sense of this world.

3. Personal rebellious tendencies to attack God when His ways are not discernable must be resisted by believers. See Chapter 2.

4. We should be thankful for the evil-conquering activity of God's Son, Jesus Christ. Because of His redemptive labors, evil will one day be expelled from the universe. See chapters 8 and 9.

Due to the direction of this study, the focus on personal evil has been limited. This does not mean, however, that it is a minor subject. On the contrary, personal evil is of great significance. It simply must be opposed by hopeful believers, who await the day when evil's Conqueror re-enters human history and makes everything right.

Appendix E

God and Tsunami[81]

Thoughts on Natural Disaster

In one of the worst natural disasters in recorded history, the 2004 Indonesian Tsunami took the lives of countless thousands of people. This particular Tsunami was caused by a magnitude nine earthquake, which yielded massive waves that eventually crashed the shores of Asia, completely leveling cites and villages. The death toll was estimated at well over 150,000.[82]

In light of such widespread devastation, many relief funds were set up, as workers scrambled to help those extremely needy people. Most of us in the West were left to pray and offer financial aid. The survivors, however, had to deal with the aftermath of this mind-boggling event.

As news groups reported the mounting casualties, and experts described what actually took place, one simple yet haunting question once again

---

[81]This appendix, which was written before the earlier sections of this manuscript, is somewhat repetitive at certain points. It is included here, however, in order to briefly address the subject of natural evil.

[82]Similarly, Hurricane Katrina, which hit the United States in 2005, was a catastrophic natural event. Indeed, its impact is nearly impossible to measure.

came to the fore: *Why?* Why would a good God allow for such utter turmoil and destruction?

It is at this point that many theists postulate that God has nothing to do with these disasters. After all, natural disasters are just that, *natural*, and so God's relationship to them is non-existent. On the other hand, some propose that evil, natural or otherwise, is simply part of the risk God took in creating a free world.[83]

But, whatever truths can be gleaned from these perspectives, those who seek to do justice to the Christian Scriptures cannot escape the tension so easily. For instance, the Psalmist declares, "The Lord has established His throne in the heavens, and His sovereignty rules over *all*" (Psalm 103:19, my emphasis). Likewise, Paul states that God "works *all* things after the counsel of His will" (Ephesians 1:11, my emphasis). Furthermore, certain passages of the Bible deal directly with the issue of God and His relationship to the natural world. In a prophecy against the city of Tyre, God allows the "ocean depths" to flood the land (Ezekiel 26:19-21). Of course this is a specific case of judgement, and so we must be careful about presuming to know God's intention(s) in any particular catastrophe. Still, the thought remains that God can indeed bring about such weather anomalies, including acts of retribution.[84] More to the point, other passages of Scripture point to the overarching control of God over nature. "Praise the LORD from the earth, you great sea creatures and all ocean depths, lightning and hail, snow and clouds, stormy winds that do his bidding" (Psalm 148:7-8). Amos even describes the Lord as the One "who made the Pleiades and Orion and changes deep darkness into morning, Who also darkens day into night, Who calls for the waters of the sea and pours them out on the surface of the earth, The LORD is His name" (Amos 5:8).

---

[83]Some take a view that might be described as deistic; in such a scheme, God "gets the whole thing started" and then pretty much takes a hands-off approach to the world. This position is incompatible with a Christian worldview, which affirms that God is very much involved in daily affairs. Then, there are the so-called open-view theists, who maintain that God took a deliberate risk in choosing to create such a world as ours. Proponents of the "open view" have drawn attention to a number of issues that traditional evangelicals often minimize. Still, while they have something to add to the discussion, they do not, in my opinion, take seriously enough the more obvious implications of divine sovereignty in Scripture.

[84]Indeed, the greatest flood that this world has ever known was specifically an act of judgment against rebellious humanity. See Genesis 6-7.

Clearly, though often mysteriously, God governs the affairs of this world, even the natural world. How, then, can we make sense of natural disasters? In what way is it possible to believe in a God who is both sovereign and good? Put bluntly: How can a gracious and ruling God allow for such evil and not be held accountable for it? Once again, we are faced with the age-old problem of evil.

What follows are a number of general remarks regarding the dilemma of suffering. My modest goal is to provide a context for thinking through human tragedy from a biblical perspective. Among many factors, I would suggest the following:

God and Human Tragedy

1. It is essential to be humble in the presence of a sovereign God.

While it may be perfectly natural, even understandable, to blame God for the awful things that take place in this world, events like the Indonesian Tsunami, it is also imperative to recognize that we stand in the presence of an awesome and transcendent God. Though a certain type of "complaining" is warranted (Psalm 55:17), it is important never to trivialize the One to whom we offer our complaints. If the Lord truly does, in some sense, control nature, then He is indeed a powerful being, far exceeding our ability to exhaustively comprehend. In light of the fact that God is the king of heaven and earth, in view of His awesome holiness and incomprehensible ways, we must never minimize His greatness. He is loving beyond words, to be sure, but He is also mighty beyond description.

2. While God is sovereign, the expression of His sovereignty clearly goes beyond what we currently know about Him and His relationship to natural events.

Though God is the Ruler of all things, including nature, we must not presume that we understand how He accomplishes this. Certainly, He works through secondary causes and other factors; that much is clear.

Beyond this, however, there is much that we cannot even begin to penetrate. God may rule in human affairs, but the "how to's" are difficult, if not impossible, to trace out. While this may not get God "off the hook," so to speak, it does help us to see that there is a vast difference between believing that the Lord rules and comprehending the manner in which He carries out His will. At the very least, and in the context of the Bible's overall depiction of God as good and fair, this factor helps us to recognize that God is never guilty of any injustice or impropriety when bad things happen, even when this may *appear* to be the case. The problem, therefore, is not God's but ours. Divine greatness combined with human ignorance leave us in a place where we simply cannot perceive all that God is and does.

3. In many ways, the existence of suffering actually demonstrates the accuracy of the Bible, which has always predicted this type of world.

While this doesn't lead to anything like a resolution to life's difficulties, it does show that the Bible, which is the primary resource for knowledge about God, contains not only hard truths, truths that are difficult to understand, but also elements that perfectly fit the world in which we live. In other words, while the God of Scripture may be beyond full human explanation, many of the things He has revealed are consistent with life (and death) as we know it. Far from disproving or invalidating God, Scripture actually provides reasons to believe that He knows what He's up to, even if we cannot grasp many of the details.

4. In considering the mystery of suffering, it is important to acknowledge and embrace the even greater mystery of the transcendent-immanent God.

One of the most puzzling features about God is the fact that He is described in Scripture as both above us and with us. On the one hand, He transcends human beings. He is thus presented as the Ruler of human history, the Governor of human affairs, and the Master of nature. It is in this sense that we must not disconnect God from daily happenings. While we may not know the manner in which He reigns, God certainly does–in His goodness and wisdom–guide all of life.

On the other hand, this same God is also immanent, that is, He is with us. In this sense He shares in our joy and our misery. He rejoices in our triumphs and sympathizes with us in our heartaches. Indeed, He is the closest of companions, the Lord who walks along side us as a friend.

What is most strange, of course, is that these seemingly opposite traits coexist in the same divine being. Yet, this is precisely the way they are portrayed in Scripture, and the biblical authors do not hesitate to place these truths side-by-side. To provide just one example, consider the scene of Lazarus' death (John 11:33-44). In that passage, Jesus clearly determines what will take place (He anticipates Lazarus' death and subsequent resurrection), yet when He arrives at the tomb He expresses genuine sorrow (He truly lives in the moment). It's as if Jesus planned the whole thing and also reacted to it. He participates in the story He creates!

The realization that God is both above and with us ought to help us get our bearings when it comes to the problem of tragedy. Again, though not resolving the difficult issues, this does help us to recognize that any resolution to the problem of evil is hidden in the even greater mystery of the transcendent-immanent God. Think, for example, of Job, who suffered indescribably. Job never received an explanation for his trials; rather, he encountered a God who, amazing at it may sound, was even greater than the untold sufferings of His servant (Job 38-42). In the final analysis, then, we are left not with complete answers but with the Answerer, who, we are told, is reliable and trustworthy. When unable to fully grasp, we can at least marvel.

Seeing the Big Picture

To be honest, situations like the recent Tsunami bother me. While I have general thoughts about the issues of God's sovereignty as it relates to human suffering, I do not anticipate anything like a final solution to the problem of evil, at least not in this life.

However, I do think it is important to have a framework, a place from which to think through these difficult matters. Whether I have hit the right themes here may be debatable, but the fact that we must start somewhere in our approach to human tragedy is unavoidable.

What I am proposing is that the Bible's vantage point be taken seriously, and this necessitates faith. By faith, I do not mean a "blind leap in the dark," as critics often accuse. Nor do I intend to enumerate with precision the content of this faith. But I do believe (there goes that faith factor again) that the general flow of Scripture provides a reasonable way ahead. And this involves a willingness to see as much as we can about the God who claims sovereignty in human affairs.

But this, I sense, is where some critics fail to be fair. While noting the apparent inconsistencies of a Christian worldview, they are less apt to pay attention to (or even be aware of) those aspects of the faith that are, shall we say, more faith-bolstering.

Among these, Scripture plainly teaches us many amazing things about ourselves and the world in which we live. For example the Bible predicts a world that includes certain positive human traits, and this is exactly what we find. On the other hand, human evil is consistent with Scripture's depiction of life in a world that has rebelled against its Creator. Indeed, this dichotomy, this strange mixture of good and evil in man, is itself an indicator that the biblical authors got it right so many centuries ago. It can be argued, in fact, that no major religion so captures the nuances of life in the real world as the Christian (and Jewish) Scriptures.

Then, of course, there is Jesus. The manuscript support for the writings that tell us of Him are substantial. The documents of the New Testament are ancient and reliable, originating, it would appear, among those who knew Him best. And the resurrection, the central factor in determining Jesus' identity, rests on solid historical evidence. That Jesus' tomb was found empty on Easter morning, that He was seen alive again by numerous reputable individuals, including some skeptics, speaks volumes about the assertion that He actually conquered the grave.[85] Beyond this,

---

[85]Former skeptic Frank Morrison wrote: "There may be, and, as this writer thinks, there certainly is, a deep and profoundly historical basis for that much disputed sentence in the Apostles' Creed–'The third day he rose again from the dead.'" Frank Morrison, *Who Moved the Stone?* (Grand Rapids, MI: Zondervan Publishing House, 1971), 193. Even Anthony Flew, the former atheist who recently changed his mind about the existence of God, admitted that "The evidence for the resurrection is better than that for claimed

many have found in the Gospels a portrait of Jesus that is believable. In other words there is much more here than a mere religious tale. There is something about Jesus that has resonated with countless millions down through the centuries.

The point of all this is not to discount the problem of evil or to minimize the horror of a Tsunami. These things will always stretch our faith and defy our understanding. However, as bad as these things are (and they are!), this is not the only part of the story. When the problem of evil tempts us to abandon faith, we must remind ourselves of *the reality of good*, the amazing influence of Jesus down through the ages, and the countless stories of changed lives.[86]

Conclusion

What could God possibly be up to amid such a catastrophe? Is this an act of judgment? A wake-up call? Something else entirely? Perhaps this is yet another example of the bizarre providence of God, which will ultimately yield fruit. Whatever theory one favors, there is likely no simplistic explanation for these cataclysmic occurrences. Indeed, I suspect there are many things that we mere mortals simply cannot apprehend; the intensity and scope of suffering in this world appear to be among them.

As we consider the many awful realities that plague this world, both from nature and humanity, our hope rests with an unchangeably good, just, loving, and yet often baffling God. Thankfully, He has not chosen to remain aloof but to live and die among us. In Jesus, the living God entered our world (to join us), encountered our sufferings (to feel for us), endured

---

miracles in any other religion." Anthony Flew, quoted in Pastors.com at http://pastors.com/article.asp?ArtID=7756. If Jesus has indeed conquered death, He is unquestionably unique among known religious figures.

[86]Among other factors that support theism, one might consider the evidence put forth by the proponents of intelligent design. See, for instance, *Mere Creation: Science, Faith & Intelligent Design*, William A. Dembski, ed. (Downers Grove, IL: InterVarsity Press, 1998), William A. Dembski, *Intelligent Design: The Bridge Between Science & Theology* (Downers Grove, IL: InterVarsity, 1999), and *The Creation Hypothesis: Scientific Evidence for an Intelligent Designer*, J. P. Moreland, ed. (Downers Grove, IL: InterVarsity, 1994).

the worst of evils (to rescue us), and in His evil-defeating resurrection gave us a hope that will outlast hard times.

One day, we will no longer be threatened by the forces of nature; one day, we will possess more information and better explanations for these heartbreaking situations; indeed, one day, Tsunamis will be subdued by the same Lord who conquered the waves nearly two-thousand years ago. Until then, let us look with confidence–shaken and baffled though we may be–to the One who comforts us in our agony, walks with us through the darkness, and promises to carry us to the light.

Bibliography

Adams, Jay. *The Grand Demonstration: A Biblical Study of the So-Called Problem of Evil.* Santa Barbara, CA: EastGate Publishers, 1991.

Atkinson, David. *The Message of Job.* Downers Grove, IL: InterVarsity Press, 1991.

Blocher, Henri. *Evil and the Cross.* Downers Grove, IL: InterVarsity Press, 1994.

_____. *Original Sin: Illuminating the Riddle.* Grand Rapids, MI: William B. Eerdmans Publishing Company, 1997.

Carson, D. A. *Divine Sovereignty and Human Responsibility: Biblical Perspectives in Tension.* Grand Rapids, MI: Baker Books, 1981.

_____. *How Long, O Lord?-Reflections on Suffering and Evil.* Grand Rapids, MI: Baker Books, 1990.

_____. *The Gagging of God: Christianity Confronts Pluralism.* Grand Rapids, MI: Zondervan Publishing Company, 1996.

Clark, Gordon. *Religion, Reason, and Revelation.* Philadelphia, PA: Presbyterian & Reformed Publishing Company, 1961.

Clark, Kelly James. *When Faith is Not Enough.* Grand Rapids, MI: William B. Eerdmans Publishing Company, 1997.

Dembski, William A. ed. *Mere Creation: Science, Faith & Intelligent Design.* Downers Grove, IL: InterVarsity Press, 1998.

_____. *Intelligent Design: The Bridge Between Science & Theology.* Downers Grove, IL: InterVarsity, 1999.

DiCello, Carmen C. *Dangerous Blessing: The Emergence of a Postmodern Faith.* Eugene, OR: Wipf & Stock Publishers, 2005.

Evans, C. Stephen. *Why Believe? - Reason and Mystery as Pointers to God.* Grand Rapids, MI: William B. Eerdmans Publishing Company, 1996.

Fee, Gordon D. *Paul's Letter to the Philippians.* Grand Rapids, MI: William B. Eerdmans Publishing Company.

Feinberg, J. S. "Theodicy" in *Evangelical Dictionary of Theology,* ed. Walter A. Elwell. Grand Rapids, MI: Baker Books, 1984.

Ferguson, Sinclair. *Deserted by God?* Grand Rapids, MI: Baker Books, 1993.

Frame, John M. *Apologetics to the Glory of God: An Introduction.* Phillipsburg, NJ: Presbyterian & Reformed Publishing Company, 1994.

_____. *The Doctrine of the Knowledge of God.* Phillipsburg, NJ: Presbyterian and Reformed Publishing Company, 1987.

Geivett, R. Douglas and Gary R. Habermas, eds. *In Defense of Miracles: A Comprehensive Case for God's Action in History.* Downers Grove, IL: InterVarsity Press, 1997.

Grenz, Stanley J. *A Primer on Postmodernism.* Grand Rapids, MI: William B. Eerdmans Publishing Company, 1996.

Jones, E. Stanley. *Christ and Human Suffering.* New York, NY: The Abington Press, 1933.

Kreeft, Peter. *Making Sense Out of Suffering.* Ann Arbor, MI: Servant Books, 1986.

Ladd, George Eldon. *A Commentary on the Revelation of John.* Grand Rapids, MI: William B. Eerdmans Publishing Company, 1972.

Lewis, C. S. *The Problem of Pain.* New York, NY: Simon & Shuster Publishers, 1962.

McLaren, Brian D. *The Church on the Other Side: Doing Ministry in the Postmodern Matrix.* Grand Rapids, MI: Zondervan Publishing House, 2000.

Montgomery, John Warwick, ed. *Evidence for Faith: Deciding the God Question.* Dallas, TX: Probe Books, 1991.

Moo, Douglas J. *James.* Grand Rapids, MI: InterVarsity Press, 1997.

Moreland, J. P. ed. *The Creation Hypothesis: Scientific Evidence for an Intelligent Designer.* Downers Grove, IL: InterVarsity, 1994).

Morrison, Frank. *Who Moved the Stone?* Grand Rapids, MI: Zondervan Publishing House, 1971.

Myers, Joseph R. *The Search to Belong: Rethinking Intimacy, Community, and Small Groups.* Grand Rapids, MI: Zondervan Publishing Company, 2003.

Newbigin, Leslie. *Proper Confidence: Faith, Doubt, and Certainty in Christian Discipleship.* Grand Rapids, MI: William B. Eerdmans Publishing Company, 1995.

Newman, Robert C. ed. *The Evidence of Prophecy.* Hatfield, PA: Interdisciplinary Biblical Research Institute, 1994.

O'Brien, Peter T. *The Epistle to the Philippians.* Grand Rapids, MI: William B. Eerdmans Publishing Company, 1991.

Pinnock, Clark, et al. "Practical Implications" in *The Openness of God: A Biblical Challenge to the Traditional Understanding of God.* Downers Grove, IL: InterVarsity Press, 1994.

Plantinga, Cornelius. *Not The Way It's Supposed To Be: A Breviary of Sin.* Grand Rapids, MI: William B. Eerdmans Publishing Company, 1986.

Smith, Chuck Jr. *The End of the World As We Know It: Clear Direction for Bold and Innovative Ministry in a Postmodern World.* Colorado Springs, CO: WaterBrook Press, 2001.

Stackhouse, John G. Jr. *Can God Be Trusted?: Faith and the Challenge of Evil.* New York: Oxford University Press, 1998.

Sweet, Leonard. *Postmodern Pilgrims: First Century Passion For the 21st Century World.* Nashville, TN: Broadman & Holman Press, 2000.

Tiessen, Terrance. *Providence and Prayer: How Does God Work in the World?* Downers Grove, IL: InterVarsity Press, 2000.

Yancey, Philip. *Disappointment with God: Three Questions No One Asks Aloud.* Grand Rapids, MI: Zondervan Publishing House, 1988.

_____. *Rumors of Another World: What on Earth Are We Missing?* Grand Rapids, MI: Zondervan Publishing House, 2003.

Credits

John M. Frame, *Apologetics to the Glory of God: An Introduction*, Presbyterian & Reformed Publishing Company, 1994. Reprinted by permission of P&R Publishing Company.

Henri Blocher, *Evil and the Cross*, InterVarsity Press, 1994. Reprinted by permission of Inter-Varsity Press Ltd. (World rights except North America)

Taken from *Evil and the Cross* © 1994 by Henri Blocher. Published in 2004 by Kregel Publications, Grand Rapids, MI. Used by permission of the publisher. All rights reserved. (North American rights)

If you would like to contact Carmen DiCello, he can be reached at
carmen1978@comcast.net

www.ingramcontent.com/pod-product-compliance
Lightning Source LLC
Chambersburg PA
CBHW060346100426
42812CB00003B/1144